101

THINGS YOU SHOULD KNOW ABOUT

SCIENCE

STERLING
New York

An Imprint of Sterling Publishing
387 Part Avenue South
New York, NY 10016

ISBN 978-1-4549-1045-9

Distributed in Canada by Sterling Publishing
c/o Canadian Manda Group, 165 Dufferin Street
Toronto, Ontario, Canada M6K 3H6
Distributed in the United Kingdom by GMC Distribution Services
Castle Place, 166 High Street, Lewes, East Sussex, England BN7 1XU
Distributed in Australia by Capricorn Link (Australia) Pty. Ltd.
P.O. Box 704, Windsor, NSW 2756, Australia

For information about custom editions, special sales, and premium and corporate
purchases, please contact Sterling Special Sales at 800-805-5489 or
specialsales@sterlingpublishing.com.

For Pulp Media Limited:
AUTHOR: Sonia Mehta (in association with Quadrum Solutions)
SERIES ART DIRECTOR: Allen Boe
SERIES EDITOR: Helena Caldon
DESIGN & EDITING: Quadrum Solutions
PUBLISHER: James Tavendale

IMAGES courtesy of www.shutterstock.com

Manufactured in China

2 4 6 8 10 9 7 5 3 1

www.sterlingpublishing.com

101

THINGS YOU SHOULD KNOW ABOUT

SCIENCE

STERLING
New York

INTRODUCTION

Science extends beyond classrooms and laboratories; it is a field that is literally as vast as the universe! It's impossible to set any limits to this subject as it keeps extending with time. Most modern advancements are somehow related to science. In a way, science sustains itself and develops itself. With new inventions, discoveries and theories, the scope of science continuously increases.

Look around your home and you'll see machines that make everyday life easier. Out on the street you'll see cars buzzing past you. These too are scientific marvels.

In this book, we explore fascinating facts about science and its different branches that you probably won't find in school books. You will read about the different types of sciences, how science has evolved, great discoveries, and of course, how science affects our daily lives. We also introduce you to great scientists and their amazing discoveries, which have helped us to understand our vast and wonderful universe.

Sit back and enjoy this journey through the wondrous world of science that will leave you pleasantly surprised!

ECLIPSE

MAMMALS

DINOSAURS

COMETS

CONSTELLATIONS

UNIVERSE

SUN

EARTH

SCIENCE AND EXISTENCE

STARS

TIME

THE SOLAR SYSTEM

COMETS

1. THE BIG BANG

Most astronomers believe that the universe was formed during an event called the Big Bang. Thus, the Big Bang Theory is the scientific explanation behind the birth of our universe. This giant explosion occurred 10-20 billion years ago – and you thought your grandparents were old!

denser than anything we know of. Then, a huge explosion occurred, which we call the Big Bang. This giant explosion threw matter in all directions in the form of a huge wave that is expanding even today!

Scientists have gathered a lot of evidence and information about the universe. They used these observations to develop a theory called the "Big Bang Theory." The theory states that around 13.7 billion years ago, the entire universe was like a tiny bubble. It was hotter and

Scientists aren't exactly sure about how the universe evolved after the Big Bang. Many believe that as time passed and matter cooled, atoms began to form into planets, stars, and galaxies. The universe includes everything we can touch, feel, sense, measure, or detect. It includes all living things, planets, stars, galaxies, space, light, time, and all matter.

FAST FACT . . .

Scientists can only predict the age of the universe within a band of 74 million years – it may have happened at any time during this period.

FAST FACT . . .

It takes eight minutes for sunlight to reach the Earth. Imagine how far we are from the Sun and therefore how vast the universe is!

FAST FACT . . .

With technology, we can see leftover background radiation from the Big Bang. This has allowed us to draw an actual map of what the Big Bang looked like.

2. OUR UNIVERSE

Space is an infinite and unknown world. The universe is a huge wide-open space that holds everything from the smallest particle to the biggest galaxy. The size of the Universe and the number of galaxies it hosts is still unknown.

The Milky Way has around 250 billion stars and astronomers state that there are 100 billion other galaxies in the universe. The Milky Way is best seen on clear moonless nights. It usually appears as a luminous light band in the sky. What we can see with the naked eye makes up less than 10 percent of the mass of the Milky Way. Can you imagine how vast it is?

The Galaxy consists of a bar-shaped core region surrounded by a disk of gas, dust, and stars within which they are organized in an oval, spiral shape. Outside the main spiral are about 200 ball-shaped clusters of stars, called globular clusters, which contain up to one million stars. All the components of the Galaxy revolve around the strong gravitational pull of the

nucleus (the center). All of these components orbit the nucleus and are held together by gravity.

The Milky Way belongs to a cluster of at least 40 galaxies. The rotational period of the Milky Way is about 200 million years and it is estimated to be about 13.2 billion years old.

FAST FACT . . .
There are an infinite number of celestial bodies floating around in space! Roughly 3,000 of these pieces are satellites, the rest are large pieces of debris.

FAST FACT . . .
The universe contains billions of galaxies, each containing millions or billions of stars!

FAST FACT . . .
Astronomers believe that the center of the Milky Way is a massive black hole. A black hole is a region or area in space where gravity is so strong that even light cannot escape from it. It is a common belief that a black hole can swallow not only planets but entire galaxies as well.

3. THE SOLAR SYSTEM

Have you ever wondered about what lies beyond the vast sky? Far above the dark horizon lies a mysterious world which was born around 13.7 billion years ago. This mysterious world is the Milky Way, a galaxy that contains our solar system.

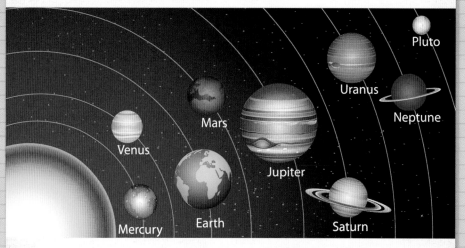

Our solar system is a small yet integral part of a galaxy known as "The Milky Way. "The solar system consists of eight planets, their moons, and all the celestial bodies that float between them. Listed in order of their distance from the Sun, the eight planets are: Mercury, Venus, Earth, Mars, Jupiter, Saturn, Uranus, and Neptune. The Sun's strong gravitational pull holds Earth and the other planets in place. Our solar system takes approximately 225 million years to revolve around the galactic center.

Our own evolution depends upon the evolution of the solar system.

Ancient astronomers believed that the Earth was the center of the universe, and the Sun and all the other stars revolved around the Earth. In the 16th century, a scientist named Copernicus proved that Earth and the other planets in our solar system orbit the Sun. His accurate theory is called "Heliocentricism."

The creation of our solar system took place billions of years before there were any people around to witness it.

Copernicus

FAST FACT . . .
Pluto
Since its discovery in 1930, Pluto was classified as a planet. However, in 2006, it was discovered that Pluto was only one of several large bodies in the solar system. Now, Pluto is classified as a dwarf planet.

FAST FACT . . .
So what's a huge star?
There are stars known as red supergiants that are over 2,500 times larger than the Sun. And those are just the ones we know about!

4. EVOLUTION

We've often heard about how our ancestors were apes. How do you think we came upon that fact? Let's find out by understanding a little about evolution!

Evolution is the process by which different kinds of living organisms develop and diversify from their earlier forms. Biological evolution is an important process, which takes place over millions of years. During this time, organisms evolve so that they are better adapted to their environments.

Some theories state that the human race is the final product of the evolutionary process, while others state that evolution is still incomplete. Rather, it is a continuing process which has been changing and forming life on Earth for billions of years. It will continue to do so for as long as organisms are born, dying, and competing for what they need to survive and reproduce.

The story of human evolution began almost six million years ago.

It describes the very long process that ultimately made human beings what we are today. This process has been understood through the study of fossils and understanding the Theory of Evolution. This theory is not yet concluded as new fossils are discovered on a daily basis, unveiling newer chapters in this amazing story of evolution!

FAST FACT . . .

Scientific research proves that Earth is the only planet in our solar system with a climate suitable for hosting various life forms!

5. 3ʳᴰ ROCK FROM THE SUN

We're usually more interested in the third planet from the Sun, as it happens to be our home planet! The Earth, our world, was formed out of hot gas almost 4.54 billion years ago. Of course, it looked nothing like the world we live on today. One of the most important things about Earth is the fact that it has an atmosphere, which is what allows it to sustain life.

Saturn is 80 percent larger than the Earth. However, if the two planets were to be dropped into an ocean, Earth would sink right to the bottom while Saturn would happily float on top. This is because of Saturn's density, which is 1/10ᵗʰ that of Earth and 2/3ʳᵈ that of water.

Since Saturn's density is less than that of water, it won't sink.

Apart from this, even though Saturn is the second largest planet in the solar system (after Jupiter), its gravitational pull is almost equal to that of the Earth. This air-headedness of

Our Solar System

Mercury

Venus

Earth

Mars

Jupiter

Saturn

Uranus

Neptune

Saturn has caused it to be called a "gas giant."

Saturn lacks a solid surface. This means that there is no land on Saturn. Its surface is a murky gaseous platform and the distinction between its surface and atmosphere isn't clear.

Aren't you glad to be living on solid ground instead of a gaseous ball?

FAST FACT . . .
Great inventions such as satellites and infrared telescopes have helped astronomers and astrophysicists to gain detailed knowledge about the Earth, as these devices enable them to view it from space!

FAST FACT . . .
Research suggests that the percentage of Earth's surface covered by water is 71.11 percent, whereas the percentage covered by land is only 28.89 percent! Therefore, it appears blue from space and is referred to as "The Blue Planet."

6. THE SUPER STAR

Many religions believed that the Earth was at the center of the universe, since it was the planet with life. Many early scientists agreed with this idea, albeit for different reasons. This model of the universe, where the Earth is at the center of our solar system, is known as the "geocentric model," and was widely accepted until fairly recently.

than the space between the Sun and the Earth. Some stars are so big that they are 1,000 times bigger than the Sun.

The Sun is a common, middle-sized, yellow star. It is a ball of hot, glowing gases. It produces

A star is a huge, luminous sphere of glowing gas. There are over 200 billion stars in the universe. The closest star to Earth is the Sun. Even though we think that the Sun is the largest star, the largest star would actually take up more

FAST FACT . . .
The part of the Sun that we see everyday is as hot as around 9,939° F. It gets hotter as you go deeper.

its own light, heat, and energy. The volume of the Sun is 1,299,400 times bigger than the volume of the Earth. Imagine how huge that is! The Sun's gravitational pull keeps the planets orbiting around it rather than drifting away aimlessly into space.

Sunlight is a crucial factor for sustaining the solar system. The Sun amounts for 98 percent of all matter within the solar system! This means that all the planets, moons, asteroids, minor planets, comets, gas, and dust would together make up only 2 percent of all the matter in the solar system.

FAST FACT . . .
Have you ever wondered what a shooting star is? It is a small, speeding meteor burning up as it enters the Earth's atmosphere.

FAST FACT . . .
A constellation is a group of stars. As the Earth turns, you can see different constellations.

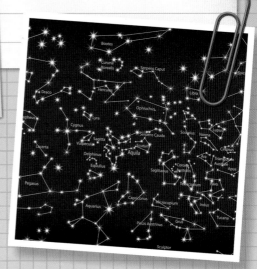

7. DAY AND NIGHT

The Earth is constantly rotating around itself as well as revolving around the Sun. This causes the 24-hour cycle of day and night.

The Sun is at the center of the solar system. The planets orbit around it at different distances. As the Earth spins on its axis, the side of the Earth that faces the Sun gets daylight, and the side that faces away from the Sun gets none, making it night-time there.

The hemisphere that points toward the Sun is warmer and gets more light – it experiences summer, while the other hemisphere experiences winter.

This effect is different near the Equator though. The Equator receives the same amount of sunlight all year round. The poles, on the other hand, receive no sunlight at all during their winter months!

FAST FACT . . .

Icy Poles
The North and South Poles are frozen for most of the year as they receive very little sunlight!

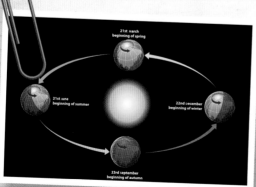

8. THE NIGHT LIGHT

The large white ball that we see in the night sky is the Moon. It has no light of its own; it only reflects sunlight and provides light to the dark side of the Earth that is not facing the Sun.

The moon does not just provide us with light at night. Its gravitational interaction with the Earth affects our weather, ocean tides, and gradually slows the planet's rotation as well.

The moon is a celestial body or natural satellite that orbits a planet. What we see today as the moon was once a part of the Earth itself. Around 4.5 billion years ago, when the Earth was just a young ball of hot lava, a giant rock from space crashed into it. This took out a chunk of the Earth and pushed it into space.

9. RUMBLING ROCKS

Asteroids, meteors, and comets are loose rock debris which float about in space. People often tend to mix their names up. But they are actually quite different from each other.

Asteroids are leftover materials from the formation of the solar system. They are large rocks floating in outer space. When they come in contact with Earth's atmosphere, they start burning. These flaming asteroids are then called meteors. Asteroids and comets are very similar, but asteroids do not have a visible tail like comets do.

FAST FACT . .
Millions of meteors pass through the Earth's atmosphere everyday.

FAST FACT . . .

Many people think that a comet's tail is always following behind it, but the coma, or tail, can either appear behind the comet or in front of it.

These rocks of debris often lose their path and crash into other planets, including our own. They not only crash on the surface but also create holes in the ground, which we call craters.

10. CAMBRIAN EXPLOSION

Life did not evolve at a constant rate over time. There have been periods where there was an explosive change in the speed of evolution. This occurred about 542 million years ago, in the Cambrian Age.

The Cambrian explosion marked the appearance of most major animal phyla. This occurred almost 530 million years ago. It was also during this time that organisms became more diverse. The first of these was marked by the appearance of vertebrates or animals that had a spinal column and a spinal cord.

Various possible reasons have been proposed for such an explosive growth. One is that the atmosphere suddenly became richer in oxygen, allowing for less fit organisms to survive, thereby aiding evolution. But the exact reason is still a huge mystery!

FAST FACT . . .

Trilobite
The Cambrian explosion marks the first appearance of trilobites, one of the first animals belonging to the arthropod class. Its name means "three-lobed" and describes the structure of these animals.

11. CLASS MAMMALIA

After the demise of dinosaurs, the world was inherited by various animals, notably mammals. Mammals are animals that are warm-blooded and give birth to their young.

Mammal babies are raised on milk secreted by their mothers from their mammary glands, which give this class its name. Another distinguishing characteristic of mammals is the presence of hair or fur on their body. Mammals are warm-blooded, which means that their body temperature is shivering. Mammals are found all over the globe – on all seven continents. They can be as tiny as mice or as large as the African elephant.

not dependent upon that of their surroundings. They can regulate their body temperature through mechanisms like sweating and

FAST FACT . . .
There are five species of mammals that lay eggs. They are called monotremes. The duck-billed platypus is one popular example.

FAST FACT . . .
Bats are often considered birds because they have wings and can fly. However, bats have hair on their body and give birth to their young – this makes them the only flying mammals!

12. DYNAMIC DINOSAURS

Imagine a giant lizard with sharp sword-like teeth as long as a man's forearm. It can run as fast as a small car and is way bigger than a truck. Terrifying, isn't it? Let's meet one.

If you've seen Jurassic Park or any other dinosaur movie, you would have thought of the Tyrannosaurus Rex after reading the paragraph above. It's the first thing that pops into people's minds when they hear the word "dinosaur."

"Dinosaur" is a word originating from the Latin term for "terrible lizard. "These creatures walked on Earth nearly 201 million years ago (during the Jurassic Period). Dinosaurs came in all shapes and sizes.

Not all of them looked like the T-Rex. They ranged from tiny ones that would fit into your palm to giants that were ten times larger than elephants!

They ruled our world for almost 135 million years, but about 66 million years ago, something happened – possibly an asteroid crash – that caused the dinosaurs to die out.

FAST FACT . . .

We still see descendants of dinosaurs today – birds. It is commonly accepted that all birds alive today evolved from dinosaurs, as did some fish.

STATIC

FORCE

MOMENTUM

MATTER

LIGHT

MASS

PRESSURE

PHYSICAL SCIENCES

MOTION

WEIGHT

HEIGHT

LAW

PHYSICS

INERTIA

13. LAWS OF MOTION

Isaac Newton was a well-known scientist who proposed the three laws of motion. He stated that these are the laws of the universe, and everything in the universe functions according to these laws.

Newton's ideas have been tested and proven so many times over the years that they are now known as Newton's Three Laws of Motion. These laws define how an object behaves with its environment. They also help us understand many daily occurrences that are unique and amazing. For example, how does an airplane fly so high in the sky? Let's understand that by taking a closer look at Newton's three laws of motion!

Newton's first law of motion is also known as "Inertia." This law states that "any object at rest will remain at rest unless acted on by an unbalanced force."

If you leave a pencil lying on the floor, it wouldn't just start moving on its own. A ball rolled on the floor comes to a stop, as does a car. But this is because of friction, the force that is created when an object rubs against something. You can see this from the fact that a ball will probably roll further on smoother surfaces than it does on rougher ones.

FAST FACT . . .
Moving Planets
Before Isaac Newton proposed these laws, we knew how planets moved, but not why. He explained the reason using his three laws of motion.

Newton's second law states that "the acceleration of a body is directly proportional to the force applied but inversely proportional to its mass." This means that if you push a door with two hands, it opens twice as fast as it would if you opened it with only one hand.

Newton's third law states that "to every action, there is an equal and opposite reaction." This law is the easiest to understand. If you bounce a ball on the floor, it will spring back up with the same force that you have applied to it.

FAST FACT . . .

Amazing Apples

Newton understood how the force of gravity and motion coincide as he sat and watched an apple fall from its tree. This made him realize that everything falls down and there had to be a reason why.

14. FORCE AND FALL

Around the 17th century, it was believed that heavier objects fell faster than lighter ones. A cannon ball dropped from a height would hit the ground before a glass marble that was dropped from the same place at the same time. However, Galileo dramatically proved that theory incorrect!

In the 17th century, Galileo Galilei dropped a cannon ball and marble from the top of the Leaning Tower of Pisa. Contrary to what people thought would happen, they both hit the ground at exactly the same time. So while Galileo proved

Galileo

Isaac Newton

that the Earth pulls all objects towards it at exactly the same rate, he couldn't explain why. It took Isaac Newton, with his Law of Universal Gravity and Second Law of Motion, to do so.

Newton's Law of Gravity established that the strength needed by the Earth to pull an object, i.e., the force with which it would pull, would solely depend upon the mass of the Earth and the object. Since the mass of the Earth doesn't change, this force is solely dependent upon the mass of the object.

If you apply the same force to a heavier object, it has less acceleration. Similarly, if you apply 10 times the force to an object that is 10 times as heavy, it produces the same acceleration. Thus, while the Earth's force of attraction might change, the speed of a falling object does not!

FAST FACT . . .
While a marble and cannon may fall at the same speed, a feather does not.
The shape of the feather makes it fall much more slowly – a fact that was used to design the parachute.

FAST FACT . . .
The force with which the Earth attracts an object is known as its weight. So while your mass remains the same on the moon, your weight becomes less than one-sixth.

15. STATIC SPARK

Have you ever received a mild shock on touching a brass doorknob? Or maybe while wearing a woollen sweater or shirt that has just come out of the dryer? Have you ever noticed a spark after scuffing a carpet? That's static electricity.

Mild shocks or sparks are often caused by static electricity. The Ancient Greeks discovered that rubbing an amber rod against wool, or a glass rod against silk, can cause static electricity. But it was Benjamin Franklin who first stated the reason behind this as a part of his experiments on electricity.

Benjamin Franklin

Rub a rubber balloon against your skin or any cloth. Then, bring it near your head and watch your hair stand on end. When you rubbed the balloon against yourself, tiny particles called electrons jumped from your skin on to the balloon, giving it a "static charge." This charge attracts your hair towards it, making it stand on end.

FAST FACT . . .

Many places, like gas storage areas, have a metal bar or plate that you must touch before entering. This helps prevent static sparks, which may actually cause an explosion.

16. ZAP!

Lightning actually helped us get electricity!
Do you find that difficult to imagine? Let's find
out how this happened.

The electricity that we use follows the same principles as static and lightning. However, unlike the latter, electricity doesn't stop after a small spark. It is a continuous flow of electrons.

Electricity was first discovered by Benjamin Franklin. He flew a kite in a lightning storm with a key at the end of it. The kite string, once wet, acted as a wire that was connected to a Leyden jar, which stored the charge it received. This established that lightning was a form of electricity.

From here on it took the work of various scientists like Michael Faraday, Thomas Alva Edison, and Nikola Tesla to bring electricity from the realm of academics into our everyday lives.

FAST FACT . . .

You may have seen a long rod on the top of tall buildings. This is called a lightning rod. It attracts lightning to it and conducts it safely into the ground to ensure that it doesn't cause any accidental damage to the building or its occupants.

Nikola Tesla

17. BOUNCE AND STRETCH

"I'm rubber, you're glue. Whatever you say bounces off me and sticks to you." If you have have heard this phrase before, you will know that rubber bounces. The harder you throw a rubber ball at a wall or at the ground, the harder it'll come back at you.

Rubber has the ability to store energy in its shape. When you stretch a rubber band, it absorbs the energy that you spent pulling it out of shape. When you release the rubber band, it uses this energy to regain its original shape.

This phenomenon is called "elasticity." You can find elasticity in various objects – cushions, foam, certain plastics, etc., all of which are elastic to a certain degree.

FAST FACT . . .
Elasticity isn't unlimited. Stretch a rubber band beyond a point and it will break. Pieces of plastic can only bend upto a certain degree before they retain the shape you put them in.

FAST FACT . . .
Certain objects' ability to store energy was known to ancient humans. They used this knowledge to make bows, which were used to fling arrows at a target.

18. FALL AND FLIGHT

There's a joke about potential energy: What's the difference between a person falling from his bed and falling from the Empire State Building? Falling from your bed is painful, but falling from the roof of a building could be fatal.

When you fall from your bed, you hit the ground before you have had the time to gather speed. This is why it doesn't hurt so bad. A building, on the other hand, is a lot taller than your bed. You already know that climbing 50 flights of stairs would be a lot more tiring than climbing two flights. When you climb upwards, gravity tries to pull you down. The energy used to work against gravity gets stored as potential energy.

And when that object falls freely, gravity converts that potential energy into moving energy or kinetic energy. Thus, you gather speed and are more likely to hurt yourself fatally.

FAST FACT . . .

Kinetic energy is the energy that an object possesses when it is in motion. It depends on the speed of the object and its mass. For example, an object moving at 50 mph has 10 times more energy than an object moving at 5 mph!

19. THERE IT GOES

Many sports, such as billiards and pool, focus on projecting one object onto another to make it move in a specific manner. Similarly, if you run into someone, you both get pushed out of your paths. This is because of something called the Law of Conservation of Momentum.

Momentum is defined as the product of an object's mass and its speed. It is a measure of how much the object would resist changing its current path. Could you stop a baseball thrown at you at 5 miles per hour? You probably can. What about a truck going at the same speed? Unless you happen to be a superhero, the answer to that question is a no.

The mass of the object and the speed at which it is traveling both determine what happens when it collides with something. If a baseball going 20 miles an hour came at you, you could stop it, even if it

stings your palm a bit. If a person going at the same speed crashes into you, you will wind up with injuries. Of course, that same person running into a wall would not injure the wall. When two objects collide, the total of their momentum before and after the collision has to remain the same.

FAST FACT . . .
Some objects absorb momentum and energy in a collision. If you punch a pillow, it doesn't really move but it absorbs most of your hand's momentum to change its shape.

FAST FACT . . .
When two objects collide, they move in a very specific pattern. The mechanics of it are rather complicated. Suffice to say that it has something to do with their shape – the way their mass is arranged. Two balls colliding would move very differently from two stars of the same size and material.

20. IMPULSE

Have you ever stopped suddenly while you were running? That's the sort of thing that makes you stumble. This is because of something called "impulse." Stopping an object with the same energy is harder when you have to do so in a short time.

On most roads, curves are gentle rather than sharp and abrupt. As we all know, if a car brakes quickly, you move forward in your seat. When you brake suddenly, a large amount of energy gets transferred to you in a very short time.

Impulse is most obviously seen in collisions when two objects touch briefly. The concept of impulse is also defined as a sudden and overpowering desire to act spontaneously.

FAST FACT . . .
Impulse also applies to bullets. A bullet with low impulse will only make a hole in a glass pane, whereas one with a high impulse will shatter it.

FAST FACT . . .
The impulse of fuel is very important in rocket science since rockets need to reach very high speeds in a very short span of time.

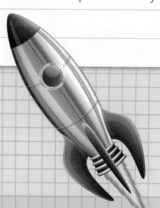

21. COLORFUL RAINBOWS

Have you ever looked up at the sky after a bout of rain to see a colorful bridge forming among the clouds? We call this a rainbow. Do you know how many colors it has? Let's find out.

We often describe a rainbow as having seven colors, but it actually has an extremely large number of colors. The normal human eye can detect seven of these most easily – VIBGYOR or violet, indigo, blue, green, yellow, orange, and red. Violet and red represent the most extreme colors we can see.

However, most of the colors remain invisible to us, only because the human eye can spot a limited number of colors!

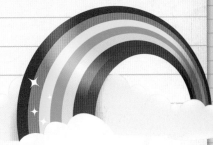

FAST FACT . . .

The phrase "being in the limelight" comes from the fact that limestone was used in the first spotlight because of the brilliant glow it gave out.

FAST FACT . . .

Many animals can see ultraviolet and infrared colors that we can't. Some animals can't see any colors and only see the world as gray.

22. SOUND ALOUD

When you plug your ears, the noise around you tends to disappear, doesn't it? The sounds of everyday life are so natural to us that their absence seems strange. But what is sound?

Sounds are waves created by objects due to their vibration. Our ears can pick up some of these sounds – which we call the "audible frequencies." The number of times an object vibrates in one second is called its frequency. Our ears can only hear objects that vibrate between 20 to 20,000 times in one second. Anything below this is called subsonic, while anything above it is termed ultrasonic.

Dogs can hear a broader range of sounds than we can. This fact is used to create ultrasonic dog whistles, which are whistles that only dogs can hear. Similarly, elephants communicate using frequencies below what we can hear, allowing them to be heard over dozens of miles.

FAST FACT . . .
No one can hear you in space
Unlike light, sound needs a medium to travel in. Space is empty; there is nothing to carry sound, so a person speaking in space cannot be heard, though he can be seen.

Sound travels as a vibration of molecules in the air. It can also travel through liquids, solids, and gases other than air. These are called the "mediums" of sound travel. The speed of sound in these different media is different. This is used in a parlor trick where people inhale helium to speak in a high-pitched cartoon voice – because helium is lighter than air, and sound travels slower in it.

FAST FACT . . .
Sound travels farther in solid objects like the ground. This helps animals like moles and rats who live underground. Their whiskers function as eyes, allowing them to sense vibrations.

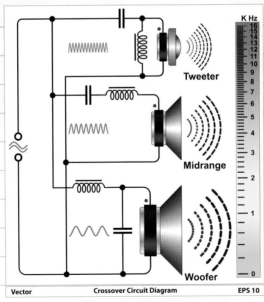

Vector   Crossover Circuit Diagram   EPS 10

Crossover Circuit

23. PUSHY PRESSURE

Like everything that is made of matter, air has mass. Because of this, it also has weight. The column of air above you is pressing down on you with its weight. This is what we call "air pressure."

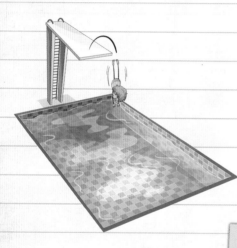

Pressure is an important function and is used in everyday life. The buttons you push on your keyboard also work along this principle.

Pressure is a measure of the force exerted by something per square inch of a particular area. Dive 10 feet deep into a swimming pool. Do you feel something pressing against your ears? That's the change in water pressure pushing against you.

FAST FACT . . .

Submarines have a maximum operating depth. It's the depth that they cannot cross. The water pressure below that level is so high that it could crush the submarine!

24. BRIGHT INTENSITY

The brightness of a place or a light source is defined as its "luminous intensity." Luminous intensity is a measure of how much light is present in an area.

Luminous intensity can be measured in a unit called "candela," which is Latin for "candle." This was originally defined as the amount of light given out by a single candle. As you may already know, not all candles glow with the same amount of light. People needed to find a more suitable way to define a standard of luminous intensity. Ultimately, luminous intensity was defined in a standard, complex way that has nothing to do with an arbitrary source like a candle.

FAST FACT . . .

All the light emitted by a source doesn't reach the destination. Technically, the light in an area is measured by something called "luminous flux" in a unit called "lumen."

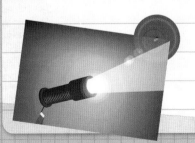

25. FIRE! FIRE! FIRE!

You may have seen a fire, but have you ever wondered about the process of burning? Why do some materials burn when others do not?

The process of catching fire and burning is known as combustion and the materials that are prone to it are known as combustible materials. When a material burns, it combines with oxygen, creating an oxide. Many oxides are commonly found as ash. Before French chemist Antoine Lavoisier proved this, it was commonly held that all combustible substances held something called a "phlogiston." When burnt, this phlogiston was released, causing combustion.

FAST FACT . . .
H_2O is the chemical formula for water. This formula denotes that water has two atoms of hydrogen and one of oxygen!

FAST FACT . . .
Rusting is also a form of oxidation! Rust is actually an oxide of the metal.

26. JUST BREATHE

The human body produces energy by oxidation, which is the burning of food! That is why we need to eat and breathe. Our blood contains a protein called hemoglobin that carries oxygen from our lungs to our cells, where it combines with the carbs and fat from our food to produce energy.

The food we eat contains many complex molecules that contain carbohydrates, fats, proteins, minerals, vitamins, and other essential food groups. The hemoglobin in our blood facilitates this process by transporting the oxygen from our heart to different parts of our body.

FAST FACT . . .

If we breathe in carbon monoxide, the hemoglobin in our blood would rather carry it instead of carrying oxygen. That's why this colorless, odorless gas is called the silent death.

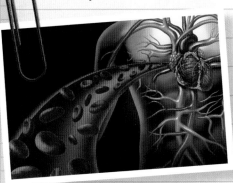

Hemoglobin is present in the red blood cells of human beings. It is vital for the transport of oxygen and nutrients to the different cells that form a part of the human body. That is why breathing is considered extremely important, as it is a primary function of the human body.

27. YUMMY YOGURT

Yogurt is created by adding previously prepared yogurt to a pitcher or bowl of milk and leaving it in a warm, dry place for a period of 12 to 24 hours. This causes the milk to change from a liquid to a thick, soft semi-solid by a process called fermentation. How does that happen?

Yogurt contains a bacteria called "lactobacillus." This lactobacillus acts on a sugar present in milk called "lactose" to convert it into lactic acid. This acid gives yogurt its characteristic taste and texture. Sometimes, milk is boiled or pasteurized to kill unwanted bacteria and prevent curdling before it is used for setting the yogurt. The amount of yogurt used to start off the process as well as the fermentation time determines the texture of the final yogurt.

FAST FACT . . .

Frozen yogurt, a popular dessert, is prepared by adding flavor along with the yogurt to the milk before setting it.

28. SAY CHEESE!

Old cameras had a roll of film in them instead of a memory card. These rolls had to be put in a dark room and washed in a solution to develop photographs. But how are these photographs taken?

Photographic film is covered in something called "photographic emulsion." It's silver mixed with other materials to form a light-sensitive layer. When the camera shutter opens, light falls on the film. Depending on what the photo is, different amounts and colors of light fall on different sections of the film. This makes the film darken to various degrees at various points, i.e., the layer changes according to the subject of the picture.

This film is then washed, treated, and enlarged on a special piece of paper to create a photograph. The film's exposure and contrast determines its quality.

FAST FACT . . .

Digital photography converts the light falling on a sensor directly into "voltage." This is then fed into a computer, which translates it back into an image.

29. REPLACING LIGHT BULBS

Light bulbs represent the first major step in modern lighting. Its impact was such that a light bulb going off in someone's head is the image of a great idea being born.

An incandescent light bulb wastes a large amount of the energy it uses in the form of heat. This has led to an increasing move to fluorescent lighting technology.

Tube lights, CFLs, and neon lights are all examples of this technology. These gadgets contain a gas, mostly mercury vapor, and a special coating, generally a phosphor.

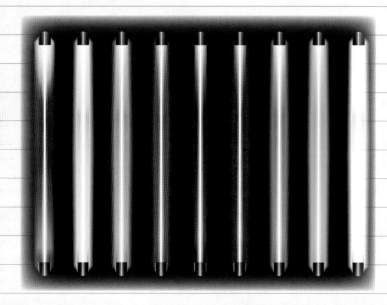

When electricity is passed through the mercury vapor, it gives off ultraviolet light.

This UV light is not visible to the human eye, but it causes the phosphor coating to "fluoresce" – a phenomenon that gives off visible light. This makes it more efficient than an incandescent lamp.

However, this is considered an environmentally hazardous practice as both mercury and phosphorous are toxic substances. Different light bulbs, such as LEDs (light-emitting diodes), hydrogen lamps, and neon lights, are used today. In fact, the developments in the field of light technology have resulted in clubs and concerts using different light displays!

The science of lighting has developed to such a great extent that it is considered to be a separate branch of scientific study altogether. Interesting lighting effects can be seen in various movies today.

FAST FACT . . .
Neon is a colorless and odorless gas. When it is filled in a vacuum discharge tube, it glows! This is how we have neon lights.

FAST FACT . . .
LED light bulbs do not have mercury or other hazardous material.

GRAVITY

HEART

BONE

ELEMENTS

PHOTOSYNTHESIS

LIFE SCIENCES

SUNLIGHT

ACIDIC

ALLOY

METALS

BASIC

30. FOOD FROM SUNLIGHT

Plants absorb light from the Sun and carbon dioxide and water from their environment to create food in the form of carbohydrates. This is done with the help of a chemical called "chlorophyll." The process of creating food in this manner is known as photosynthesis.

Photosynthesis literally means "creation from light." It mostly occurs on the leaves in centers called chloroplasts. The plant absorbs water from the soil through its roots and carbon dioxide from the air. These are combined using light energy to create carbohydrates. The waste by-product of this process is oxygen. Photosynthesis is the only reason for the presence of oxygen in the atmosphere.

This is why planting trees and increasing the green cover of areas is very important. Our growing population and industrialization destroys many trees to make way for residential, commercial, or industrial areas. This reduces the amount of trees in our environment, which disturbs the balance between oxygen and carbon dioxide.

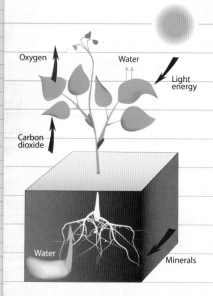

Oxygen

Water

Light energy

Carbon dioxide

Water

Minerals

A lack of oxygen can cause a lot of problems, especially to an ever-growing population. If we want the human race to survive, we must plant more trees.

FAST FACT . . .
Forests are known as the lungs of the Earth, as they let out oxygen and help us breathe.

31. REAL STEEL

The beautiful thing about elements is that you can mix and match them to get surprising results. For instance, iron is a metal that is soft and relatively weak in its purest form. Carbon is a soft, black, powdery non-metal. If you add a pinch of carbon to iron and mix it, you get steel, a hard, flexible, and silvery piece of metal ideal for many industrial applications.

Steel is known as an alloy. An alloy is a mixture of two elements, one of which is a metal. Think of it as a solution, like salt and water. The only difference in this case is that the mixture is then solidified in a way that preserves its structure, i.e., the two materials are mixed evenly throughout. Alloys often display properties that are very different from their parent components – like steel. It is also possible to create alloys for specific purposes, like being non-magnetic or resistant to acids and corrosion.

There are many different types of alloys of steel, such as the stainless steel alloy, which is capable of withstanding water corrosion. Most machines and industrial equipments are made of stainless steel due to its ability to prevent rusting, which ultimately causes wear and tear and damage to these machines.

The economies of several different countries are completely dependent on steel. As steel is a basic component in industries like construction and engineering, a fluctuation in the prices of steel can have a very major impact on such economies.

FAST FACT . . .

Damascus steel is an ancient form of steel, although the method of making it is lost to us. It had a water pattern on it. Swords made from this steel were rumored to be sharp enough to cut a hair draped over it.

32. CHEMICAL CATEGORIES

In chemistry, substances are often classified as acidic, basic, and neutral, depending on their behavior in a solvent and other criteria. Certain tests determine this quality by checking the substance's PH level or exposing it to litmus paper.

The acid and base form salt and water, water being neutral. This is important, because many applications need the solvent not be overly acidic or basic in nature. In such a case, the appropriate acid or base is added to achieve a usable solution.

Acidity, basicity, and neutrality are important indications of the nature of a substance. They are useful in many chemical reactions. Acids and bases cannot stand each other – they do not co-exist. When an acid and a base are brought together, they form a "neutralization reaction."

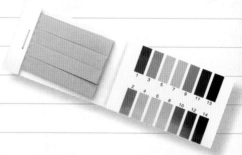

Two common examples are soap and lime. Soap will not alter the color of a litmus paper, as it is basic in nature. On the other hand, lime is highly acidic.

The litmus paper will instantly change color when it touches lime.

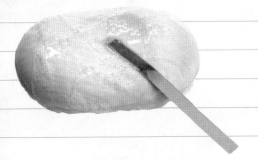

FAST FACT . . .

A litmus paper is a filter paper with dyes extracted from certain lichens. Acids turn blue litmus red and bases turn red litmus blue. This test has given rise to the commonly used phrase "litmus test."

33. SKIN

Humans and other animals often use a sense of touch or a "tactile sense." We touch objects to check for edges, curves, texture, and position. Biologists call this "somatosensory perception." It refers to various sensations like heat, tactile reception, and pain that we receive from our skin.

Our skin is the biggest organ in our body. It has a network of nerve endings that stretch under it like a giant net to capture various sensations.

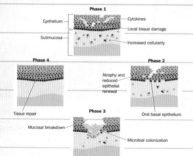

Layers of the skin

It consists of an outer layer called the "epithelial tissue." This serves as a primary barrier to foreign materials entering our bodies. Mammals have an outer covering of hair as protection on their skin, while birds have feathers, reptiles have scales, and insects/arthropods have an exo-skeleton that acts like armor.

The skin also performs various functions like letting out sweat and regulating temperature, among others.

FAST FACT . . .
Friction can burn! Certain areas of the skin grow thick and tough in response to repeated friction.

34. HARD AS A ROCK

What do human nails and hair have in common with scales, claws, and horns? They're made of the same basic material. This material is a hard, long, fibrous protein known as keratin.

Keratin is found bundled into tight coils, which give it its characteristic hardness. There are two main types of keratin:alpha keratins, which are found in the claws, hooves, nails, and horns of mammals; and beta keratins, which are found in the nails, scales, and shells of reptiles, and claws and beaks of various birds.

Scientists say that the armor plates of various dinosaurs were made of keratin. Unlike the epithelial tissue, keratin does not accommodate a network of nerves. This makes it ideal for organs that are more exposed and therefore more vulnerable to damage.

FAST FACT . . .

Most arthropods have an external skeleton of a material called "chitin." This material forms composites with different materials to give the arthropod its required properties like strength, hardness, flexibility, etc.

35. SENSATIONAL SNOWFLAKE

We may appear similar to each other in one way or another. But each of us has a unique signature - our fingerprints. They are a network of ridges raised from the adjacent skin, most prominently appearing on the pads of our hands and feet.

Fingerprints are more properly termed as "dermal papillae," which literally means "skin pimples" in Latin. They are also termed as friction ridges as they make the skin less smooth. This helps us grip objects better.

Fingerprints are a form of identification. Every individual has their own unique set. Some countries use thumb impressions as a signature. Fingerprints are also commonly used for recording the attendance in schools and colleges, and also in offices and industries.

FAST FACT . . .

A method that is gaining popularity as a substitute for fingerprint identification is "iris scanning," which scans the unique patterns of an individual's eye to identify them.

36. MORPHING

What does an organism do when it is confronted by a predator? It tries to be dangerous. Bees have stings, deer have horns, and snakes have venom. What can you do if you don't have any of these?

Many animals and plants simply pretend to be something else, either to drive away predators or to attract prey. This form of behavior is called "mimicry." Mimicry is present in various life forms for different purposes, and can protect both, the mimic and model. The model refers to the original organism while the mimic refers to the organism that copies the traits of the model.

Mimics can copy the looks, the behavior, as well as the sound and location of the model. Some common examples are insects that look like leaves. Some non-venomous snakes copy the coloring of venomous ones to avoid predators. Stray weeds sometimes resemble crops, which camouflages them and protects them from being pulled out.

FAST FACT . . .

The coral snake mimics the look of a milk snake, which is less dangerous than itself. It does so to avoid predators instead of attempting to discourage them.

37. GRAVITY AND GROWTH

Gravity has a major impact on human beings and all other objects on the Earth. It causes objects to fall when they are dropped from a height. It also keeps us grounded to the Earth. In the absence of gravity, all of us would have simply been floating!

When a person is standing up, gravity is acting on his/her spine. The spine is a collection of flat discs that rest on top of each other. When you stand up, these discs press flat against each other with your own weight pressing them down. When you lie down, the load on these discs is removed.

FAST FACT . . .

Your skeleton takes up your weight and provides a rigid frame for your body. In space, that isn't really required, so your body stops maintaining it as well. As a result, astronauts lose a fraction of their bone mass every month in space.

As a result, these discs tend to revert to their original shape and expand. The difference in the height of an average person after eight hours of sleep may be as much as half an inch! However, this is temporary.

38. BORN IN PURPLE

"Born in purple" refers to someone destined for monarchy as a result of being born to royalty. The origin of this was in Byzantium, where the royal birthing room had walls made of purple stones called porphyry. Prior to this, purple was considered a royal color due to its expense and rarity.

Syrian purple or imperial purple comes from a species of sea snails known as murex, from the family muricidae. It was used in 1600 B.C. by the early Phoenicians. This dye is special because it does not fade with exposure, but grows brighter instead.

Murex secretes this dye as a defense mechanism when attacked; this is one way to extract this dye. A more common method is to crush the snail along with the shell and extract the dye from the remains.

FAST FACT . . .

The champagne gene is found in horses. It produces distinctive golden coats and hazel eyes with freckled skin. These horses can be distinguished at birth due to their bright blue eyes and pinkish skin.

39. HYPER HEART

The heart is more than just a blood-pumping muscle for us. When we feel sad, we say that our heart aches. Right before the final 30 seconds of a basketball game, when the scores are even, we find our hearts beating faster. Our heart beats faster when we play sports, climb too many stairs, or run for a long time.

We treat the heart as a special organ. However, the cuttlefish wouldn't find it so special – mostly because it has three of them. The actual function of the heart is quite different from the function that we credit it for. Emotions are not related to the heart –they are related to our brain.

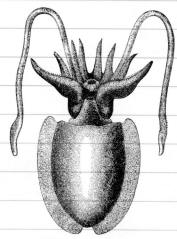

The cuttlefish is a shellfish that lives near all coasts around the world, except North and South America. Two of its hearts pump blood to its gills, one to each, while the third circulates it to the rest of the body. Cuttlefish have green-blue blood because their body uses hemocyanin instead of hemoglobin to circulate oxygen to its cells.

Hemocyanin carries less oxygen than hemoglobin, and as a

result blood has to be pumped faster and more frequently around the cuttlefish's body. This is probably the reason why it needs three hearts.

It's interesting to note how we, as human beings, never actually give importance to the heart for its real scientific reason!

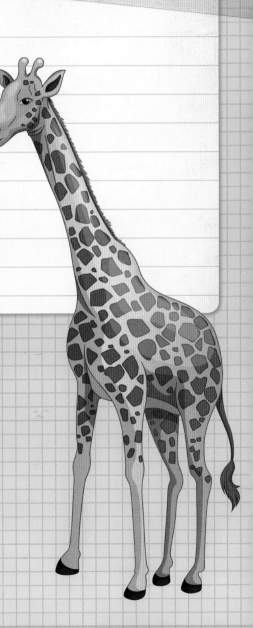

FAST FACT . . .

Giraffes have huge hearts that are around 25 lbs in weight and over 2 feet in size. Their blood pressure is twice that of a human being, with a heart beating 150 times a minute to ensure that their brain gets enough blood at the end of their long necks.

TRADITION

CELLS

ELEMENTS

LIFE

SCIENCES

ANCIENT

ADVANCED

TOOLS

PHYSICAL SCIENCES

CIVILIZATIONS

REGENERATION

ASTRONOMY

40. SCIENCE IN ANCIENT INDIA

The ancient Indians of the Harrapan civilization and the Dravidians were quite advanced. They had detailed scientific knowledge, and they were more progressive than Indians who lived centuries after them. Most of their knowledge was buried along with their civilization.

Ancient Indians were well-versed in the science of preserving grains and food in different climates. The Indian subcontinent had four well-defined seasons, namely monsoon, winter, summer, and autumn. They knew which crops suited each season, and they also knew how to look after these crops.

This civilization was well-versed in mining too; gold mining, stone quarrying, and the use of copper were extremely common during their time. A few years later, they learnt the science of polishing stones. The Ashoka pillars that were constructed during the time of Emperor Ashoka have perfectly polished stones. The gloss and polish used during those times are not available even today. Modern masons have been unable to replicate the finesse of the products used during the ancient times.

Several ancient books, such as the four Vedas, the Puranas, and other books written by great scientists of the ancient times are the treasure chests of scientific knowledge.

In fact, the "God particle" or the Higgs-Boson particle, which was discovered in 2013, was located with the help of the knowledge extracted from ancient Indian sciences. The scientists responsible for the discovery have credited scriptures such as the Rig Veda for containing information about their existence thousands of years ago.

FAST FACT . . .

The first iron-cased and metal-cylinder rockets were actually invented in India. Indian warrior Tipu Sultan used them to fight against the British in the 1780s. This science was way ahead of its time. Though he was able to ward off British attacks for a while, Tipu Sultan ultimately had to surrender to the might of the British Army.

FAST FACT . . .

The first signs of step wells in the world are actually found in India. Remains from the time of the ancient Indus Valley and Harappan civilization show that people made use of step wells to draw water from wells.

41. ANCIENT INDIAN SURGERY

The history of science credits Indians for being the first people to perform a surgical procedure. In ancient times, this meant working without anesthesia with very basic instruments. Imagine having your stomach cut open while you are fully conscious and then being stitched back together! The Indians developed a method of surgery which was very successful.

During the first century A.D., a great Indian physician named Charak was born. He later wrote a book named "Charak Samhita." Subsequently, in the third century A.D., another great Indian scientist and physician, Sushruta, authored a book named "Sushruta Samhita." Both these books are treasure troves of medical knowledge. Several European and Western books, which were written centuries later, were inspired by them.

The Sushruta Samhita

The Sushruta Samhita, which is a book written by Sushruta about surgical science, has information about over a hundred surgical

instruments – which is roughly the same number of instruments that surgeons use today!

Great Physicians

A physician named Jivaka, who was a member of Emperor Bimbisara's court, was another legendary physician. Legend says that he performed brain surgery on a merchant and cured him of his ailment. He also had advanced knowledge about different fragrances that could be used for different purposes. The education in the field of medicine was compulsory in the ancient Nalanda University, the first university of its kind in the world. Indian physicians and surgeons were given great respect all across the world for their path breaking discoveries.

FAST FACT . . .

Apart from Sushruta, Charaka was another great Indian physician.
He is known in India as the "Father of Medicine." His book, "Charaka Samhita," contains a staggering 120 chapters that discuss the most minute details about medicine.

FAST FACT . . .

Ayurveda is the ancient Indian science of medicine, which made use of natural plants, herbs, roots, oils, and parts of animals to provide treatment for various ailments, diseases, and illnesses. It is extremely popular even in modern times. Some of its methods are said to be more effective than modern forms of treatment.

42. THE MESOPOTAMIANS

Mesopotamia was a very progressive civilization. Their people were not just pioneers in science and mathematics but also influenced civilizations around them to develop an interest in these fields. They were among the first to make use of the wheel, which revolutionized the way we live. The Assyrians and their predecessors, the Sumerians, also made numerous contributions to science.

One of the greatest contributions of the Sumerians was the invention of writing. They were among the first to develop different tools which were used for writing.

The use of the wheel, which was amongst the most important inventions in the history of humanity, has been found to have first taken place in Sumeria around 3500 B.C. The wheel was used for pottery back then. Around 3200 B.C., the Sumerians had developed a detailed knowledge of science that enabled them to make chariots using these wheels. These chariots were pulled by animals like horses.

Mesopotamian astronomers followed the motion of the stars, planets, and the moon.

They could predict the movements of several different planets. Mesopotamians also invented with different pills and creams to treat various illnesses. This shows their progress in the field of medicine. They used the wheel to make pots, they discovered the process of irrigation and scientifically cultivated different crops, and also knew how to polish and chisel different weapons made of bronze and iron.

FAST FACT . . .

The Babylonians successfully discovered Earth's neighboring planet, Venus, as they saw it appear in the morning and the evening. They could also calculate the length of the Venus cycle successfully.

FAST FACT . . .

The Zodiac cycle was actually created by the Sumerian civilization. They invented constellations like Cancer, Leo, Scorpio, Gemini, Capricorn, etc., between 2000 and 3000 B.C.

43. ANCIENT GREEK SCIENCE

The Greeks, too, were pioneers in the field of science. They wanted to know the reason behind everything. Many great Greek philosophers and scientists did not believe in magic, myths, and religion. This made them study the fields of philosophy, science, and astronomy, which resulted in several inventions, theories, and discoveries.

The Greeks developed the science of philosophy because they wanted to understand the world around them.

They wanted to prove existent beliefs wrong by finding the correct reason behind various phenomena that occurred around the world. They were heavily influenced by the ancient Egyptians and the Babylonians. This, in turn, led to the development of Greek science.

Ancient Greek scientists and astronomers studied the known world, the Earth, seas, and mountains, and took great interest in the study of celestial bodies, the solar system, and planetary motion.

Contributions

The Greeks can be credited for the science of astronomy. They organized stars into constellations, which were then used for various practical purposes like fixing the calendar and measuring time. They were also among the first to estimate the size of the Earth.

Greek medicine was quite advanced, as they carried out studies to find out how different organs worked, and studied various diseases too. There are several ancient Greek inventions and discoveries made by geniuses like Plato and Socrates. For example, they found out that the Sun is the center of the solar system.

FAST FACT . . .

Hippocrates was an ancient Greek physician who is considered to be the "Father of Medicine." All doctors have to take the Hippocratic Oath, where they promise to practice medicine honestly and in the best interests of their patients.

FAST FACT . . .

The Almagest, which was written by Greek astronomer Ptolemy, is one of the only surviving works about astronomical bodies like the Sun, moon, and others from the ancient Greek period. It is a detailed book that talks about calculations dealing with the past as well as future position of planets.

44. ISLAMIC SCIENCE

Ancient civilizations were fascinated by planetary motions and the movement of the Sun and moon, which held a lot of significance for them. As a result, they began studying the Sun and moon with great vigor and, in the bargain, developed Islamic science.

Astronomy is embedded into the Islamic culture and tradition. Ancient Muslims used their superior scientific knowledge to come up with the first known accurate solar calendar. Muslim scientists and astronomers discovered many new stars, like Deneband Rigel. They also set up observatories and invented astronomical tablets like the Toledan tablet.

Muslim astronomers were known to have invented various instruments, including the quadrant and astrolabe, which led to the development of ocean navigation.

FAST FACT . . .

An Islamic physician named Al-Razi is credited for the discovery of smallpox. He wrote about it in his book, "Al-Judriwa al-Hasba," which released around the 10th century A.D.

45. CHINESE SCIENCE

It is widely believed that, between 600 A.D. and 1500 A.D., the Chinese were the most advanced technological society known to mankind. Their level of understanding and progress in the field of science was simply amazing.

One of the earliest Chinese scientists was ShenKuo, the first person to describe the magnetic needle compass that was used for navigation. The magnetic north, which is not exactly at the point of the geographical north, was accurately identified by him.

Ancient Chinese scientists also created a celestial atlas of star maps and constructed the first large astronomical tower. In the field of medicine, Chinese ointments, creams, and other mixtures were developed over the ages to provide a cure for numerous illnesses.

FAST FACT . . .

The art of making paper using the bark of trees is believed to have originated in China. It started during the period of the Tang Dynasty and spread from China to the rest of the world.

46. RAIN

Through the history of science, there have been several scientific theories which have been fielded by different scientists. Some of them have been quite interesting and shocking, and many have been proved wrong over the course of time.
One such theory stated that the rain was dependent on cultivation and human settlements.

Around the 1800s, many people began moving to the Great Plains in North America and settling there, based on a new scientific theory, which suggested that the amount of rain increased or decreased according to the number of people in a particular region. It also depended on the cultivation of the land.

Most people actually believed it and began settling in different arid and deserted regions like the Great Plains.
Dr. Samuel Aghey Junior, from the University of Nebraska, was one of the people who supported this theory to a large

FAST FACT . . .

Vulcan was considered to be a planet by the 19th century scientists.
They believed that this planet existed between Mercury and the Sun. Scientists searched frantically for this planet but never found it. Finally, Einstein's theory of relativity explained the motion of Mercury around the Sun and put all claims of the existence of Vulcan to rest!

FAST FACT . . .
The Earth is Expanding! Before the late 20th century, it was a widespread belief among scientists that the Earth was growing larger and larger over the course of time. However, once the study and concept of plate tectonics was introduced, this theory was proven wrong.

extent and also came up with an explanation for it. He stated that this theory was true as the soil of regions, when cultivated, behaved like sponge, absorbing moisture which then evaporated, leading to more rainfall. So, the more a region was cultivated, its chances of possible rainfall were better!

Failure and Aftermath
Another American scientist named Charles Dana Wilber came up with the famous line "the rain follows the plow," which meant that the more a region was cultivated, the more rain it would get! The theory was a complete failure as there were severe droughts in the 1890s in such regions!

47. ALCHEMY

Alchemy was considered to be a form of ancient science, where certain people believed they had powers to convert various substances into gold, apart from doing other interesting things which most people were not capable of. Belonging to a branch of scientific studies called pseudo science, several people since ancient times have claimed to be alchemists!

Pseudo science is a field that deals with the studies of different arts and practices which were believed to have been a part of science. These practices and arts are based on philosophical or superstitious beliefs that are not scientifically proven. Alchemy happens to be one of them.

Egyptian Alchemists

It is often said that the ancient Egyptians developed the field of alchemy. They knew how to make glass, cosmetics, and mortar, which they used to make gigantic pyramids.

As different civilizations of the past mingled, the Greeks and the Mesopotamians also came up with their own theories of alchemy and spent a lot of time trying to convert regular metals like copper and brass into noble metals like gold and silver, which were considered a lot more precious. They believed in a stone called the "Philosopher's Stone," which could perform this task! The alchemists performed several experiments in their quest for gold! These experiments, in turn, led to the development of chemistry.

48. EARTH - THE SPHERE

Theories about the position and shape of the Earth, Sun, moon, and other celestial bodies have undergone a lot of changes since ancient times. Many scientists from the medieval and ancient times tried to prove existent beliefs. One of these beliefs was that the Earth is flat.

A commonly held belief across the ancient world was that the Earth is flat. Ancient Babylonians, Greeks, and even the Egyptians believed that the Earth was a flat disk. The entire concept of the Earth being a sphere was not introduced till the fourth century B.C. Scientists, like Aristotle, strongly supported the fact that the Earth is a sphere.

Finally, as developments in science progressed and the subject was given more importance, it was finally proven that the Earth is a sphere and not flat. Furthermore, it was

FAST FACT . . .

19th century scientists believed that the planet Mars had a network of gullies and ravines, which were called the Martian canals. These supposed canals were quite an attraction for stargazers. Claims in this regard were rubbished when greater telescopes and advanced optical technology proved that this was merely an optical illusion.

FAST FACT . . .

Luminiferous ether was a type of ether believed to be the source of transmission of light in the Universe, right from the ancient Greek times. As more complex and scientific theories came up, this theory and ether died a natural death.

proven that the Earth is a planet which revolves around the Sun while the moon is the Earth's satellite, which revolves around it. It took humans centuries to finally come to this conclusion.

49. FOUR HUMORS

The field of biology has undergone many changes since ancient times, which has resulted in improved health and medical facilities, and an increase in the average life expectancy. An interesting belief of the ancient times was that of the "four humors," which, according to various civilizations, were the four substances responsible for the survival of human beings.

Right from the ancient times, it was believed that human beings survived due to the combination of four substances in their bodies, which were also referred to as the "four humors." These were blood, black bile, yellow bile, and phlegm.

It was believed that the correct combination of these "four humors" was responsible for the survival of human beings. If there was an imbalance of these, it would result in different illnesses and the subsequent death of human beings.

The Four Temperaments
Hippocrates, the Father of Modern Medicine, supported this theory along with other physicians of his time. They came up with the concept of

the "Four Temperaments." According to this, the mood of any individual was completely dependent on the combination of these "four humors." The four temperaments suggested were choleric, melancholic, sanguine, and phlegmatic.

Treatments in ancient times involved the purging of blood and addition of other fluids. This was supposed to neutralize the effect of one of these "four humors" to establish the correct balance. This theory was a part of biology and medicine up to the mid-1800s. In 1858, Rudolf Virchow introduced the concept of cellular pathology, which led to the end of this ancient theory!

FAST FACT . . .

Einstein believed that even though there was a lot of internal movement within the universe, it was stationary as a whole. Furthermore, the size of the universe and its volume also remained constant. This theory was proved wrong when Edwin Hubble came up with the theory of the red shift. It was one of those rare times when geniuses like Einstein made a mistake!

FAST FACT . . .

There was a field of study called "phrenology" (now considered a part of pseudoscience). According to it, characteristic traits of humans like aggression, intelligence, etc., were dependent on localized parts of the brain. If these parts were bigger, their particular trait would be more powerful.

50. CELL REGENERATION

The concept of cells being the building blocks of organisms is a very recent development in science. For centuries, this belief did not exist. Human beings had a bizarre theory behind the evolution of various organisms.
Cell regeneration is now recognized as a crucial part of the human body.

In the absence of microscopes, which are only a recent development, human beings did not know about the smaller structures that combined to result in our physical appearance. People did not know about cells, which are the basis of biological studies in modern times. Man had no concrete theory to back his origin and that of various other organisms, except for one bizarre theory!

FAST FACT . . .

Lizards can recreate parts of their body. This is because their cells regrow at a rapid rate. If their tail is cut off, it will grow back!

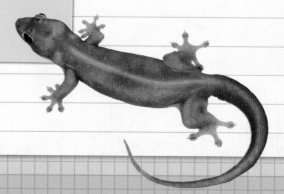

FAST FACT . . .

According to the Miasmatic Theory, diseases such as cholera and plague were caused by a "miasma," which meant pollution in ancient Greek. This was considered to be a form of bad air. This concept was not washed away until the late 1800s, when the germ theory of diseases grew popular.

Some philosophers, like Greek philosopher Anaximander, believed that human beings originated from the soil, which is why we eat herbs, vegetables, and fruits from it to survive! These beliefs were not limited to ancient times but existed well up to the early 1800s. In fact, some scientists even came up with recipe books for making animals. These were, of course, unsuccessful! Finally, in 1859, scientist Louis Pasteur proved that this theory was absolutely incorrect.

The Theory of Spontaneous Generation

According to this theory, man believed that life arose from non-living objects. He also came up with different non-living and inanimate matter from which different living organisms arose. For example, maggots were spontaneously formed from rotten meat according to this theory! Human beings were believed to have originated from dust.

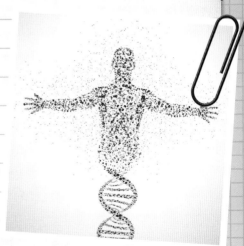

51. MATERNITY

Another very common belief was that a baby's birth depended on how a mother behaved during her pregnancy. Many mothers were held responsible for the deformities or handicaps that their children faced, and were often shunned by people. With the progress of science, this theory was proven incorrect.

The supposedly scientific theory of maternal impressions is an extremely old belief held by different civilizations across the world. According to this, the thoughts and emotions of a pregnant woman largely decide the special characteristics that her child is born with. Due to this belief, several pregnant ladies were always kept comfortable and satisfied. Any unpleasant situation that made the mother feel sad, scared, or depressed would have a direct impact on her child and its characteristics. If the mother suffered from any particular fear, it was believed that the child would also suffer from a similar fear. This put a lot of pressure on pregnant women back then!

The Elephant Man

Joseph Merrick was an Englishman born with terrible deformities. His skin was similar to that of an elephant, which led him to be nicknamed as "The Elephant Man." As people widely believed in the theory of maternal impressions, they thought that these deformities were seen in Joseph because his mother was scared of elephants. The rise of the genetic theory in the 20th century completely eradicated this theory, which had led to such incorrect beliefs for so many years! Pregnant women could actually breathe a sigh of relief, thanks to the genetic theory.

FAST FACT . . .

The medical condition of peptic ulcers was a common occurrence in the 20th century. Doctors initially credited this to the stress of modern-day life. In the 1980s, an Australian clinic discovered that the reason for these peptic ulcers was actually a certain type of bacteria. Did you know that bacteria can actually grow inside our bodies? How gross is that!

52. THE FIFTH ELEMENT

Since the ancient times, it was believed that four classical elements formed almost every single object in the world. These were earth, water, fire, and air. However, in the mid-1600s, a German physicist suggested the existence of a fifth element.

The theory of the four basic classical elements dominated scientific studies in ancient times. However, German physicist Johann Joachim Becher completely turned the scientific world upside down in 1667. He stated that apart from these four classical elements, there was a fifth element that existed in every substance with the ability to burn. This element was called "phlogiston," and it was believed to possess no color, no mass, no odor, and no taste. When substances burned, it was believed that this element was released, leaving behind a powdery substance known as calyx (which we know today as oxide).

FAST FACT . . .

In the mid-1800s, many scientists, including Lord Kelvin, believed that the Earth was only 20-40 million years old – which they considered quite young! However, geologists like Charles Lyell and biologists like Charles Darwin proved this assumption to be incorrect. Today, it has been proven that the Earth is about 4.55 billion years old.

Lavoisier's Discovery

Becher believed that objects and substances that burned brightly in air were extremely rich in phlogiston. Furthermore, this theory also stated that since fires were extinguished when oxygen was removed, it was clear that oxygen could absorb only a limited amount of phlogiston.

FAST FACT . . .

Vitalism was a scientific theory which stated that the functions of living beings were controlled by a "vital force and not by biophysical means." However, the discovery of DNA by Watson and Rick in 1967 resulted in the complete dismissal of this theory!

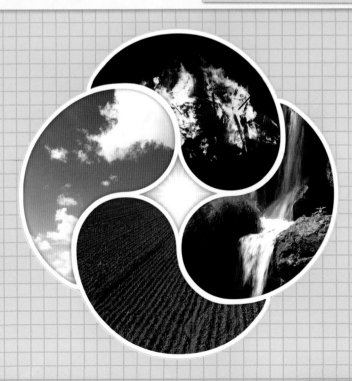

53. BLANK SLATE THEORY

In the long list of scientific theories that were ultimately proved wrong, "tabula rasa" or the blank slate theory is very important. The development of the brain was incorrectly explained using this theory for many generations. However, it can be credited for detailed studies into the brain's functions, which led to modern theories and the development of different fields of biology.

"Tabula rasa," which means blank slate, was a very important scientific theory used to explain the development of a child's brain for hundreds of years until the science of genetics and DNA was discovered in the 1900s.

According to this theory, a child is born without any knowledge about his/her surroundings or anything in the world. In other words, the child's brain is like a blank slate. The brain has no content and learns only from experience and perception. The child's personality, social and emotional behavior, and intelligence are determined by his/her experiences and perception of the world. Aristotle, the Greek philosopher and scientist, was the first person to put forth this theory. However, it was forgotten for thousands of years after he stated it. Later, in the 11th century, Islamic scholar IbnSina established this theory, which came to be widely accepted. However, as science progressed, the field of genetics was born and the tabula rasa theory was proved to be completely wrong. This is because genes and other hereditary traits are acquired by children at birth. Additionally, innate instincts, which are also inbuilt, play an important role in the development of children.

FAST FACT . . .

American electrochemist Stanley Pons and British chemist Martin Fleischmann performed a type of nuclear fusion called cold fusion at a much lower temperature as compared to hot fusion. There was a sudden craze about it and many scientists tried to replicate it. However, they were unsuccessful and it was never replicated!

VACCINATION

INVISIBILITY

PERIODIC TABLE

RELATIVITY

ATOMIC NUCLEUS

GOD PARTICLE

PENICILLIN

VITAMINS

GRAVITY

DISCOVERIES THAT CHANGED THE WORLD

ELECTRICITY

HYBRID

54. ALEXANDER'S PENICILLIN

It is difficult to imagine a world without antibiotics. They are quite important, and are responsible for providing the cure to most deadly illnesses affecting the human body. Most of these diseases had no cure in the early 1900s, but the discovery of penicillin changed that.

antibiotic properties. He decided to call this "penicillin."

The Uses of Penicillin
Since the discovery of penicillin, this medicine has been used to cure several diseases in the past, such as syphilis and infections caused by other bacteria. Until its discovery, infections and diseases caused by various bacteria were not curable and frequently fatal.

The scientist who can be credited for the discovery of penicillin is noted Scottish scientist and Nobel Laureate, Alexander Fleming. He discovered that when the bacteria "Penicilliumruben" was grown correctly, it would give out a substance that possessed

Alexander Fleming was not really looking to discover a cure, though. He discovered penicillin accidentally! Fleming had a laboratory in the famous Imperial College of London. One day, he once left a culture of bacteria in a petri dish open by mistake. He noticed that the bacterium was contaminated by a blue-green mould that formed a visible growth. He then decided to conduct a proper detailed experiment that enabled him to study this visible growth in detail. Later on, this came to be known as penicillin. Thus, we can credit the cure for various diseases to a very fortunate laboratory accident!

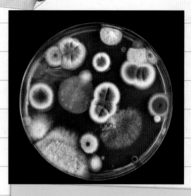

FAST FACT . . .

In the 1860s, when Louis Pasteur began experimenting with bacteria, he found out the source of diseases. He discovered that they were caused by micro-organisms, which could be killed by using heat and disinfectants. He used this theory to come up with his legendary process of milk treatment to kill bacteria, and called it "pasteurization."

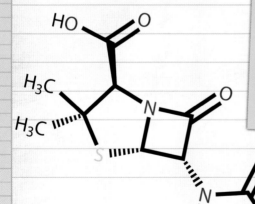

55. JENNER'S VACCINATION

Until the early 20th century, smallpox was a deadly virus that led to the death of millions across the world. There was no cure in sight. Several people tried bizarre practices to rid themselves of smallpox. However, none seemed to work. Then, a smart British physician developed the practice of vaccination, which led to the complete eradication of this deadly disease.

Edward Jenner was a British physicist who made it his life's mission to find a viable cure for smallpox. He wanted to put an end to the menace that claimed a million lives around the world. He made an interesting observation when he realized that dairy maids from his hometown often caught cowpox from the cows they looked after. This was a milder version of smallpox that spread from cows and could be easily cured. However, what astonished him was that these dairy maids seemed to develop an immunity

FAST FACT . . .

In modern times, AIDS has become a deadly virus that has resulted in the deaths of millions of people around the world. In 1983 and 1984, Luc Montagnier and Robert Gallo discovered that AIDS was caused due to the HIV virus. Since then, people suffering from AIDS have been treated with vaccinations, and are tested often. This may one day lead to the cure of this disease.

caught cowpox and was easily cured of it. After this, Edward Jenner injected him with the smallpox virus. He realized that his body was completely immune to it and did not react to its presence in any way. This led to the development of a vaccine.

The development of vaccination started from there and today, we have vaccinations for various deadly diseases.

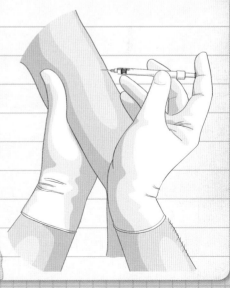

towards smallpox.

He then decided to conduct an experiment. He injected a young boy named James Phipps with the fluid oozing out of one of the sores of a dairy maid who had caught smallpox. The boy

56. VITAMINS

People often tell us to have vitamins, because they are a very important part of our diet. Many diseases and illnesses are caused by various vitamin deficiencies. People of ancient times suffered from such diseases when the entire concept of vitamins and other nutrients wasn't known to them. Their discovery was a monumental step in science.

Since ancient times, it was a well-known fact that eating certain kinds of foods could protect human beings from different diseases. For example, in the 19th century, a Scottish doctor discovered that eating citrus fruits could prevent scurvy.

Over the next few years, scientists and physicians, such as Nikolai Lunin of the Soviet Union (now Russian Federation) and F. Gowland Hopkins of England, performed different experiments to identify the vital nutrients that prevented such diseases. An experiment was conducted by feeding a set of mice with two different kinds of milk – one possessing such nutrients and one not possessing them. They were regarded as vital to the human diet and came to be known as vital amines, which eventually altered to "vitamins." The existence of these nutrients was established around 1920. Several different vitamins were then discovered, such as Vitamin A, B, C, D, E among others. Each of these were a vital part of our diet, and worked to prevent different diseases. That is why we are asked to take our vitamins!

FAST FACT . . .

The deficiency of Vitamin B1 in human beings results in a disease called "beri-beri," which causes weight loss, body weakness, irregular heart rate, brain damage, and ultimately death. It is very important to have vitamin B1, also called thiamine. It is commonly found in grain husks.

FAST FACT . . .

The deficiency of Vitamin C causes a disease called scurvy. It makes people suffer from lethargy, bleeding gums, skin spots, loss of teeth, fever, and ultimately death. Vitamin C can be obtained by eating citrus fruits. Sailors who did not eat fruits for extended periods of time often suffered from scurvy.

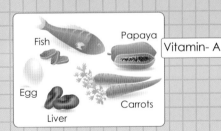

Vitamin- A

Vitamin- B

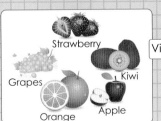

Vitamin- C

Vitamin- D

57. INVISIBILITY CLOAK

An invisibility cloak is a clothing accessory that everybody dreams of, but only Harry Potter possesses. Just imagine possessing such a cloak and sneaking out of a particularly boring class or simply spooking a friend out by appearing out of nowhere!

Until 2012, scientists belonging to various parts of the world had been trying tirelessly to create Harry Potter's invisibility cloak. However, Harry and his friends seemed to be the only ones capable of owning an actual one! There were several obstacles that had been coming in the way of creating an actual invisibility cloak. But in 2012, after numerous failures, researchers from Duke University finally tasted success when they created a "flawless" invisibility cloak that would give Harry Potter's cloak a run for its money!

Metamaterials

Metamaterials are man-made and have the ability of completely bending light, so they do not allow reflection. These metamaterials are responsible for scientists achieving the illusion of complete invisibility!

Scientific Phenomenon

Everything that we see is because of the reflection of light. The light enters our eyeballs through our pupils. The colorful circle around the pupil is called the "iris," and that controls how much light is let in.

A "flawless" invisibility cloak has special scientific properties that make it so unique. Ordinary materials do not appear invisible due to the optical phenomenon of reflection. In order to create a perfect invisibility cloak, scientists had to work towards completely stopping the phenomenon of reflection. Therefore, even though the invisibility cloak is not exactly what we see in sci-fi movies, a realistic version of it does exist today.

At present, the invisibility cloaks have been able to achieve perfect invisibility in only one direction. However, this is a tremendous scientific breakthrough. So don't lose hope, maybe we can all own an invisibility cloak someday in the future!

58. THE GRAVITY APPLE

You may have heard people say, "An apple a day keeps the doctor away." Apart from being extremely good for health, the apple can also be credited for one of the most monumental discoveries in the history of science. It can be credited for being the inspiration behind Isaac Newton's discovery of gravity and its effect on the Earth.

One fine day, a scientist, physicist, and mathematician named Isaac Newton sat under an apple tree to work on a complex theorem or study a scientific theory, just like he usually did. All of a sudden, an apple fell off the tree and landed on Newton's head! This apple must have been really special, because it opened up Newton's brain. Instead of worrying about the lump on his head, it made him wonder about how different objects moved at different speeds on Earth and what affected their direction of motion.

Knowing well enough that his predecessors, like the great Galileo, had carried out experiments and research about this, he decided to build on their research. He studied how the universe functioned and, based on his studies, he came up with the concept of gravity and the laws of motion of different objects on the Earth. He also calculated this force and compared it with the force

FAST FACT . . .
In healthy human beings, insulin is secreted from the pancreas and helps balance blood-sugar levels. However, for diabetic patients, the insulin secretions are incorrect. This results in an imbalance in blood-sugar levels. The development of lab-created insulin has helped diabetic patients in a very large way, as it now helps them balance their blood sugar levels.

FAST FACT . . .
The discovery of the Rh factor and different types of blood groups has been one of the most important discoveries, as it has helped save several lives during childbirths and operations. Before this, blood transfusions often turned out to be fatal due to incompatible blood groups. However, the Rh factor completely solved this problem.

required for that lucky apple to fall from the tree onto his head. He found out that these two forces were the same, which led him to develop the entire concept of gravity.

59. ELECTRICITY

There is a lot of debate about who actually discovered electricity. Unfortunately, the real person responsible for its discovery might never be known, but there are a lot of indications that electricity was discovered in ancient times. The development of electricity has been extremely important in the development of life, as it is difficult for us to imagine life without electricity!

The ancient Greeks knew about electricity. They knew that when amber was rubbed with fur, these two objects were attracted to each other. This was over two thousand years ago!

During the 17th century, scientists made numerous discoveries, including the invention of the electrostatic generator, distinction between conductors and insulators, and the concept of positive and negative currents.

In the early 18th century, American scientist Benjamin Franklin established the relation between electricity and lightning using a kite. While the kite was flying, it was struck by lightning, which further led to the development of the concept of electricity. The term electricity is derived from the

FAST FACT . . .
The discovery of the alternating current by Nikola Tesla is hailed as one of the most important discoveries ever. Alternating currents (ACs) are more easily transmissible as compared to direct currents (DCs).

Greek word "elektron," and was coined by William Gilbert in 1600 to define the force that was created when two objects were rubbed against each other.

Michael Faraday and Electromagnetism

English scientist Michael Faraday made two major discoveries related to electricity and magnetism that totally changed the course of our lives. He discovered that when a wire carrying an electric current is placed in front of a single magnetic pole, it causes the wire to rotate. This discovery led to the development of the electric motor. Ten years later, he discovered the electric generator as well.

FAST FACT . . .

In 1869, American inventor John Wesley Hyatt discovered how to produce a substance that has become a part of our daily life – plastic. Today, plastic is so important that we cannot imagine life without it. It truly was a monumental discovery!

60. THE MANHATTAN PROJECT

One of the most significant discoveries in the history of science and radioactivity has been the development of nuclear power. It has caused devastating results, and yet, has also been used effectively for peaceful purposes across the world. The atom bomb, as we know it, is simply a form of nuclear power.

At a time when World War II was at the very pinnacle of destruction, a set of the world's best scientists were holed up in a laboratory in New York. They were trying to figure out how to refine uranium, from which nuclear bombs like the atom bomb are made. This secret mission is also referred to as the "Manhattan Project." Their mission was successful and they were able to come up with the world's first atomic bombs, which were then used to end the war. This was done by dropping the atomic bombs on Hiroshima and Nagasaki.

The death and destruction they caused was so massive that their after-effects are felt in Japan even today. It made Japan surrender immediately and that ended World War II. In modern science, this is one discovery that most certainly has changed the world.

After atom bombs were used for the first time, scientists saw the level of destruction that was caused. They suggested that nuclear power should only be used

FAST FACT . . .

In 1905, American scientist Bertram Boltwood learnt that the age of a rock could be identified based on the amount of lead-206 and uranium-238 in the rock. Using this method, it was possible to find out how old the world actually is.

for peaceful purposes, like generating electricity through nuclear reactors. It has been used for this purpose from then on. However, nations have continued to build nuclear weapons that are used as symbols of power.

61. THE UNIVERSE'S BIRTHDAY

Until the 1920s, very little was known about the universe. There was no scientific proof to back the theories presented to explain its formation. The universe, like everything else, had to possess a beginning. However, the origin of the universe was a matter of great debate among philosophers, astronomers, and scientists. This debate finally came to an end in 1927.

Various experiments and research in the field of astronomy and physics had proved beyond doubt that the universe had a beginning.

In 1927, thinkers finally came to a consensus on the origins of the universe. Belgian astronomer Georges Lemaître came up with the concept of the Big Bang Theory. According to this theory, the universe came into existence about 13.7 million years ago when a massive explosion took place. Before this moment, which is called "The Big Bang," the universe did not exist and was simply a tiny dot.

In the fraction of a second, this dot expanded and filled the entire expanse which now forms a part of the universe as we know it. There are many scientific observations that have supported this theory.

Over time, it was believed that the universe continued to fragment, resulting in the formation of different planets, satellites, and many other celestial bodies.

The concept of the Big Bang Theory also led to the development of the Black Hole Theory. The Black Hole is believed to be a vast hole with such a major gravitational pull that everything gets sucked into it and loses its characteristics.

FAST FACT . . .
The universe has about 2,000,000,000,000,000,000 stars! These stars cluster together and make up galaxies.

62. THE DNA DUO

In February 1953, a significant discovery in the history of biology took place the discovery of DNA. Scientists were successfully able to find out the structure of the chemical patterns that are responsible for the characteristics of various human beings. This discovery has resulted in human beings understanding the concept of genes and making attempts to artificially create various hybrid creatures.

Until the early 1900s, it was only known that children bear several resemblances to their parents. It was also known that people belonging to a certain community or race had various physical resemblances. For example, most people from Africa were dark and well-built, and people of South East Asian origin had distinct physical features, such as their eyes.

What was not known scientifically is why this actually occurred. On February 28, 1953, James Watson of the United States and Francis Crick of England were successful in making one of the greatest scientific discoveries in history – DNA, which stands for Deoxyribonucleic acid.

Watson and Crick also determined the structure of DNA, which was two strands twisted around each other to form an endless variety of chemical patterns that created instructions for the human body to adhere to. We possess genes that are passed on from one generation to another.
The genes are made of chemical substances called DNA that determine the color of our hair and eyes, and other physical characteristics.

FAST FACT . . .

Some species possess such well-developed DNA that it doesn't really break down. It results in them becoming ageless. There are different species of lobsters and turtles that have been found to possess such DNA, which actually helps them live for hundreds of years!

The discovery of DNA has led to the development of a branch of biology, referred to as genetics.

FAST FACT . . .

British scientist Rosalind Franklin was the first to produce x-ray diffusion pictures of DNA, which had a huge impact in Crick and Watson's discovery. However, she died early and could not qualify for a Nobel Prize.

63. THE PERIODIC TABLE

From the time of alchemists, the science of chemistry has undergone several developments. The discovery of newer elements has been an important step in the development of chemistry. The development of the periodic table in its modern form has been largely responsible for the discovery of the properties of different elements.

The periodic table is an arrangement of different elements possessing similar properties in an orderly manner. This development in the field of chemistry has been largely responsible for the discovery of a host of different elements. of elements that possess similar properties. Using this arrangement, missing elements in the periodic table have been discovered, based on the properties of the elements surrounding their position in the periodic table.

Modern Periodic Table

The Modern Periodic Table was developed by English physicist Henry Moseley in 1913. He realized that arranging elements in the order of their atomic numbers (the number of protons they possess) results in a regular pattern

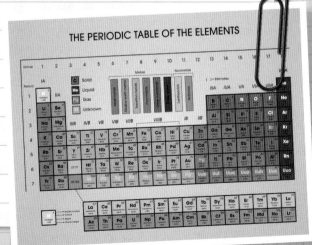

THE PERIODIC TABLE OF THE ELEMENTS

The History of Elements

Various attempts were made to arrange the elements of the periodic table. Chemists

FAST FACT . . .

The first ten elements in the periodic table are hydrogen, helium, lithium, beryllium, boron, carbon, nitrogen, oxygen, fluorine, and neon. They are found to have certain similarities due to their positions in the periodic table.

FAST FACT . . .

The noble gases appear in the last column of the periodic table. Helium, Neon, Argon, Krypton, Xenon, and Radon are noble gases. They are special because they are highly uncreative and extremely stable.

like Johann Dobereiner from Germany and John Newlands from England came up with possible options that failed in the long run. When Russian chemist Dmitri Mendeleev tried organizing elements in the order of their atomic weights, it was fairly accurate and almost the same as the Modern Periodic Table.

However, the arrangement in the order of atomic numbers turned out to be the most apt and accurate method. Even though there are some inconsistencies, it has been effective in most cases and has led to the discovery of numerous elements.

64. THEORY OF RELATIVITY

Among the numerous different discoveries and theories that were put forward by Albert Einstein, the most famous one is the Theory of Relativity. It redefined many laws of physics. This eccentric genius in 1905 redefined the way things looked, as well as our perception of how they moved.

The Theory of Relativity is too complicated for us to understand in complete detail. It was, of course, developed and presented by Albert Einstein, who is said to be the smartest man to have ever lived. Though his theories have impacted various spheres of science and mathematics, it is this theory that literally redefined an entire branch of physics.

The Theory of Relativity explains the relationship between speed, time, and distance. It also defines the concept of a frame of reference. It was because of the Theory of Relativity that the speed of light was determined to be constant. Until then, it was believed that the speed of light was variable and depended upon different circumstances, such as the relative position of bodies. But the Theory of Relativity was able to prove

that the speed of light always remained the same, and was 300,000,000 m/s.
This was not impacted by how fast or slow a particular body was moving towards or away from something.

The Theory of Relativity established the basis for modern sciences and studies like radioactivity, quantum physics, and many others. Imagining the world without Albert Einstein and his Theory of Relativity is a very difficult proposition!

FAST FACT . . .
Among the numerous eccentricities that Einstein was known to have, one of the weirdest ones was that of not wearing socks. He never wore socks because he thought that they were a pain and developed holes.

$$Speed = \frac{Distance}{Time}$$

65. THE X-RAY MEN

German physicist Wilhelm Röntgen was the real x-ray man. His crucial discovery of x-rays resulted in the birth and development of a completely new concept in the fields of security and medicine. You will realize the importance of this discovery when you come to think of the fact that every single airport or train station that you visit is kept secure thanks to x-rays.

X-rays were popularly referred to as Röntgen rays. They have truly made the world a much safer and healthier place. Even Wilhelm Röntgen would not have realized their significance when he first discovered them during one of his experiments in 1895. Once the discovery was established, he won the Nobel Prize in Physics in 1901.

X-rays are electromagnetic waves with a special wavelength capable of penetrating certain substances like human flesh and wood, but not materials such as bones and lead.

As a result, when the human body is exposed to x-rays, it penetrates the human flesh but not the bones and provides an impression of the bones.

The X Factor

X-ray systems have revolutionized the field of medical treatment. Through their use it is much easier to penetrate the human flesh and identify accurate areas where a fracture has occurred.

X-ray systems are commonly used for security purposes all over the world. When bags and other prices of luggage are passed through them, they can detect any dangerous or sharp objects by providing their image. If you ever decide to commit a crime, know that x-rays are going to catch you in a jiffy!

FAST FACT . . .

X-ray detectors are secretly placed in strategic locations such as crowded places in big cities to detect any possible attack or explosion that is planned and avert it. This method has been very effective and x-rays have saved many parts of the world from destruction!

66. ATOMIC NUCLEUS

The discovery of atoms was a significant step in the development of various sciences. Since atoms are extremely small in size it is difficult to carry out research on their nature and structure. However, the discovery of the atomic nucleus was the first step in this direction and opened a lot of doors for further study. An atomic nucleus consists of electrons, neutrons, and protons.

New Zealand physicist Ernest Rutherford was responsible for discovering the structure of an atom. He had earlier discovered two types of rays in radioactivity, namely alpha and beta rays. He found out through his earlier research that alpha particles were positively charged and when they were placed on a screen, a sharp and clear image was obtained. However, if a thin sheet of mica was placed between the screen and the alpha ray source, a slightly diffused image was obtained. This made them realize that the mica sheet was definitely scattering some particles and they decided to find out the reason behind this.

In 1911, Rutherford carried out further experiments by placing a thin sheet of gold foil and focusing alpha particles on them. He found out that a diffused image was formed on a certain part of the gold sheet and alpha particles were reflected from these regions. He came to the conclusion that there was a strong positive charge at the center of the gold atoms. This charge was responsible for this phenomenon. He called this strong positive source the "nucleus," and he inferred that it was quite small as compared to the atom's size.

FAST FACT . . .

The size of the nucleus is much smaller than that of an atom. It would be interesting to note that the size of the nucleus is literally 100,000 times smaller than the size of an atom. When you realize that atoms are among the smallest structures known to mankind, you'll understand how small it actually is!

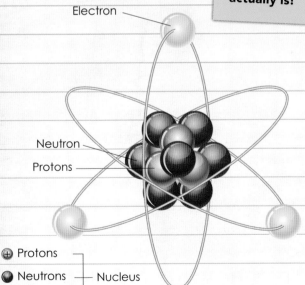

Electron

Neutron

Protons

⊕ Protons ⎤
● Neutrons ⎬ Nucleus
⊖ Electrons ⎦

67. THE GOD PARTICLE

The Higgs Boson or the "God Particle," which was discovered in early 2013, is one of the most significant discoveries in modern times. Hundreds of scientists from all over the world came together to try and discover this particle and prove its existence at CERN in Switzerland, where a special reactor was set up for this purpose.

The results of this discovery are so far reaching that it threatens to redefine various branches of science. The Higgs-Boson particle is considered to be one of the most important building blocks in the universe. It explains the reason due to which sub-atomic particles such as protons and electrons have mass. Another reason due to which this discovery is considered so important is that it brought together scientists from across the world to collaborate on such an important discovery.

The reason why this particle is considered so important and is also referred to as the God particle is that it touches every other particle and is responsible for giving them different mass. The Higgs field is the one in which all particles are believed to interact. The heavier particles have greater interaction with it while the weaker particles have much lesser interaction. Hence, the Higgs-Boson particle is considered fundamental to the existence of the universe.

A lot of research is still being carried out into how it can be used. Scientists are working on understanding how it can be applied to different fields in the world. The mass and other properties of the Higgs-Boson particles are being determined in a step-by-step manner.

FAST FACT . . .

Scientists who discovered the "God" Particle have largely credited ancient Indian science for this discovery. They stated that theories about the existence of such a particle were provided in ancient Indian scriptures and they really helped in the final discovery of the Higgs-Boson particles at CERN.

PRIESTLEY

GALILEO

DARWIN

KEPLER

DALTON

ARISTOTLE

EDISON

EINSTEIN

SCIENTISTS WHO
CHANGED THE WORLD

VOLTA

NEWTON

68. THOMAS EDISON

Thomas Alva Edison is among the most revered American scientists and inventors of all time. Known to have held over 1050 US patents and several other UK patents in his name, he revolutionized the telecommunications industry. However, it would be difficult to determine how much of his success would have been possible without "power naps!"

Childhood and Early Life

Born in Milan, Ohio, Thomas Edison grew up in Port Huron, Michigan. Quite contrary to popular belief, he wasn't considered the smartest student in school. In fact, his teacher considered him to be "addled"–which literally means "a rotten egg!" However, he certainly showed his talents after school.

His Famous Inventions

Edison's first major and recognized discovery was the phonograph, an instrument that was capable of recording sounds. Back then, people thought it was magical and he was called a magician.

This resulted in him being renowned as "The Wizard of Menlo Park."

His most notable inventions include the carbon microphone used in telephones until the early 1980s, the earliest motion picture camera, and of course, the electric bulb!

His Famous "Power Naps"

Edison took short "power" naps in the armchair, with his hand supported by the elbow, while tightly holding a bundle of balls in this hand. He believed that this stimulated his subconscious mind to work on his inventions. When he fell into a deep sleep, the bundle of balls would fall and the noise would wake him up.

He would then start writing whatever was on his mind, which was usually the solution to a problem! Who would've thought that taking naps would be a solution to problems?

69. AMAZING ARISTOTLE

The ancient Greeks were brilliant scientists. They invented amazing things, some of which are still of great importance to our lives. Among the numerous philosophers and scientists, one of the most well-known ones was Aristotle.

FAST FACT . . .

Aristotle rightly determined that the Earth was round. However, he also thought that the Earth was stationary and was at the center of the universe.

Belonging to a lineage of philosophers and scientists, Aristotle contributed to numerous fields of science, philosophy, and even politics. Aristotle's name stands strong among the most well-known philosophers and scientists of all time. He had vast knowledge about a variety of different disciplines, right from poetry to zoology to politics!

Aristotle was among the most influential people in Greece during his times. He was born in Stagira, ancient Greece, in

384 B.C. He contributed greatly to different fields like physics, poetry, zoology, logic, rhetoric, politics, government, ethics, and biology. He became a part of the Greek aristocracy at the age of 18 and was tutored by another renowned Greek philosopher, Plato.

Aristotle spent his entire life researching different natural sciences. His research in the

FAST FACT . . .
Aristotle spent a lot of time studying biology. He was the first to classify animals into different groups. He wrote several books including "The Natural History of Animals" and "The Parts of Animals."

field of astronomy helped to establish several facts about the motion of the Earth, Sun, moon, and other celestial bodies. He carried out massive research in the branches of pure science like physics, chemistry, and astronomy.

70. SURGICAL SUSHRUTA

Ancient India has been a huge contributor in the field of science. Scientists and physicians practiced methods thousands of years ago, which were only rediscovered in modern times. Among the renowned scientists of ancient India was Sushruta, the first surgeon known to the world. A genius of his times, he laid the foundations for the medical science of surgery long before any other civilization had even dreamt of it.

Sushruta lived around the sixth century B.C. He was a surgeon who authored the "Sushruta Samhita," which is still considered one of the most important books in the history of medicine.

He lived in Varanasi, India, and is believed to have practiced his surgical procedures on the banks of the river Ganges. Sushruta performed complex surgeries such as the cataract, caesarean, plastic surgery, and even cosmetic surgery.

FAST FACT . . .

In 1827, British surgeon Joseph Lister developed sanitized surgical techniques that were clean, without any bacteria and germs. 50 percent patients who underwent surgery back then used to die because of bacteria and germs. The development of the Antiseptic Surgical Technique by Lister resulted in surgery becoming a much safer method of treatment.

FAST FACT . . .

Actresses and models who get nose jobs done to make their noses look more attractive can thank the great Sushruta for having developed this form of surgery. Today, a nose job is one of the most popular procedures among women.

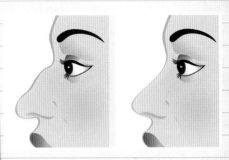

In fact, he divided surgery into eight broad categories. He is believed to have been the inventor of cosmetic and plastic surgery, by using a flap of skin from the forehead to restructure disfigured noses.

Sushruta also developed over 650 drugs of animal, plant, and mineral origin. He taught people the art of surgery by making them carry out surgical procedures on inanimate objects like reeds and watermelons. These were the first surgical workshops ever conducted in history.

He was a living, breathing medical dictionary of sorts and is revered in medical science as the "Father of Surgery."

71. JOSEPH PRIESTLEY

Oxygen, which is a lifeline for all of us, was discovered in the late 1700s when Joseph Priestley came across it during one of his experiments. This English scientist, who spent the later part of his life in the North America, made several other contributions to the field of science. His most important discovery was oxygen.

Joseph Priestley was born in Leeds in 1733. He was the son of a cloth-dresser. After his mother died when he was just seven years old, he was brought up by his aunt. He was a brilliant student. Local teachers in Leeds helped him become proficient in physics, algebra, and many different languages.

Priestley was very interested in the study of science and how it could benefit the human race. Being a man with a variety of interests, he also developed an interest in politics. He wrote several articles and a book on political systems.

He moved to North America later, and his research was supported by many renowned American scientists, such as Benjamin Franklin. In the 1770s, he began research on the properties of gases. He learnt how to prepare carbonated water, which led to

The most important of all these gases was, of course, oxygen. He also contributed to the theories of photosynthesis and respiration.

Priestley's discoveries greatly influenced various developments in the field of chemistry.

the development of the soda industry. He called the different gases "airs" that were released from a variety of substances.

Priestley designed an apparatus and used instruments smartly to isolate eight different gases.

72. ALBERT EINSTEIN

You've probably heard about Albert Einstein at some point in your life, just like every student who studies science. In fact, the word "Einstein" is used to describe geniuses. Albert Einstein has also been declared in many different polls as one of the greatest men to have ever lived on our planet. What makes this man the most brilliant mind we have ever come across? Let's find out.

FAST FACT . . .

After the first President of Israel, Chaim Weizmann, passed away in 1952, the Prime Minister of Israel offered the job to Albert Einstein. However, Einstein politely declined the offer.

Quite frankly, Albert Einstein does not need any introduction. It is said that he used his brain four times more than any of us have ever done. Born in Ulm, Germany, in 1879, Einstein traveled around the world and came up with many different theories. The most famous of these is the "Theory of Relativity". He came up with both special and general theories for the same. He received the Nobel Prize for Physics in 1921 for his interpretation of the photoelectric effect.

Einstein was born into a secular Jewish family in 1879. An interesting thing to note about Einstein was that he was a failure in school. Apart from physics and mathematics, he did not like a single subject and often failed. Einstein received honorary doctorates from several different European and North American universities. His knowledge in later years spread beyond the scope of physics and mathematics alone. His approach to solving problems in physics was quite unique. No one in the same field has been able to replicate them. In fact, his approach and theories were often so complicated that high-level scientists and physicists found them very difficult to understand!

73. ALESSANDRO VOLTA

Alessandro Volta is among the greatest Italian physicists of all time. His research and study was extremely influential in the development of the electric battery. It was around his time that the age of electricity had just begun. Hence, he is considered to be one of the founding fathers of the electric age. Having spent most of his life studying electricity and the various phenomena associated with it, he developed the voltaic piles that could generate steady currents.

Alessandro Volta was born in Como, Italy, in 1745. He was a brilliant child and his family initially sent him to a Jesuit school in the hope that he would become a Jurist.

FAST FACT . . .

Alessandro Volta was known all over the world, not only by scientists of his time but also by political heads for his discoveries, theories, and inventions. French ruler Napoleon Bonaparte felicitated him in 1801 by calling him to Paris and giving him a special gold medal. Volta's full name was Alessandro Giuseppe Antonio Anastasio Volta.

The First Battery – The Voltaic Pile

Constructed out of alternating discs of copper and zinc, the voltaic pile also consisted of cardboard dipped in brine solution between two alternate discs. This voltaic pile was capable of producing a very steady electric current and came to be known as the first battery that had ever been developed. It also had a metallic conducting arc, which was used to carry the electricity over much larger distances. A unit of electromotive force, which is called the Volt, has been named in honor of his achievements.

He became a professor of the Royal School in Como in 1774. In the same year, he came up with his first invention, the electrophorus – a device capable of generating static electricity. He studied electricity at the University of Como for years, igniting static sparks of electricity and studying their nature.

When he moved to the University of Pavia, where he worked as a professor, he came up with his most famous discovery – the Voltaic Pile.

74. SIR ISAAC NEWTON

Sir Isaac Newton, President of the Royal Society and Member of the British Parliament, is most famously remembered as the man who discovered the Law of Gravitation by looking at a falling apple.

Newton finished his initial schooling at The King's School, Grantham, before moving to Trinity College, Cambridge, as a sort of teaching assistant. It was during this period that Newton first created his generalized binomial theorem and started his work on calculus.

Born on Christmas Day, December 25, 1942, in the English county of Lincolnshire, Isaac was named after his father, Isaac Newton, who passed away three months before Newton's birth. His mother remarried and moved in with her new husband, leaving Newton with his grandmother.

Once Trinity College closed because of the plague, he returned home. This was the period where his genius really began to shine and he discovered the Law of Universal Gravitation.

After this, his career took flight, and he made great advances in the fields of classical mechanics,

FAST FACT . . .

Newton's epitaph, as composed by Alexander Pope, reads: "Nature and Nature's laws lay hid in night; God said 'Let Newton be' and all was light."

the end of this period, he'd split the visible spectrum of light, written his book "Principia Mathematica," and established classical mathematics.

This ended abruptly in 1693 when he suffered a nervous breakdown. In his later life, Newton became religiously and politically active, holding the offices of Member of Parliament and Warden of the Royal Mint until his death in 1727.

optics, and mathematics. This was when his great argument with Gottfried Wilhelm Leibniz began, which ended only with the latter's death in 1716. Their row was over who had invented the infinitesimal calculus. Though Newton is thought to have won the argument, we use Leibniz's version of notations in calculus today. By

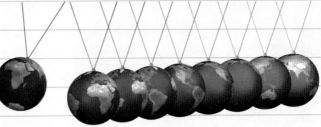

75. ANTOINE LAVOISIER

Antoine Lavoisier, as he was known later, was born Antoine-Laurent de Lavoisier as a nobleman in France. He is often touted to be the father of modern chemistry. He transformed chemistry from a speculative theoretical science to a quantitative science that used a definitive system of weights and measures, and quantitative theory.

Laurent Lavoisier.

It was here that his interest in the sciences was aroused. At age 26, he bought a share in the French taxation system, effectively becoming a tax collector. He tried to introduce monetary reforms in the system and helped develop the metric system to standardize weights and measures.

Lavoisier was born as the scion of a rich noble family in Paris on August 26, 1743. He studied at the College Mazar, also known as the College of the Four Nations, in Paris, from 1754 to 1761.

In 1772, Lavoisier turned to the phenomenon of combustion, working on its mechanism. He disproved the phlogiston theory of combustion and explained the mechanism of oxidation.

He also identified oxygen, hydrogen, and sulfur, and predicted the existence of silicon. He worked in the royal gunpowder commission, an assignment that earned him a private laboratory. He began practicing stoichiometry – proving that reactants react in very specific quantities based on their molecular structure. Lavoisier's life was disrupted greatly around 1789 when the French Revolution gained force. Despite his best efforts to dissociate himself from it, he was arrested on November 24, 1793, as a former tax collector. He was tried, convicted, and summarily executed by guillotine on May 8, 1794.

FAST FACT . . .

Upon hearing of Lavoisier's death, Joseph Louis Lagrange said, "The head that they cut off in an instant might not be reproduced given a hundred years."

76. CHARLES DARWIN

Charles Darwin, Fellow of the Royal Society, was born on February 12, 1809. Born the fifth of six children in a wealthy doctor's family in Shrewsbury in 1809, Darwin was raised by his eldest sister from the age of eight. At a very early age, he displayed an interest in insects and minerals, showing a scientific curiosity and experimentation. He was enrolled at the Edinburgh University to study medicine, but proved too faint-hearted to become an able physician.

In 1831, a naturalist was needed to travel on a scientific expedition – a voyage around the world in the brigantine HMS Beagle under the supervision of Captain Fitzroy. Darwin's fellows at Cambridge, where he had barely earned a degree in theology, recommended him and he got the job. Over the course of the five-year voyage he collected the bones of extinct animals and studied living ones in their habitat.

He observed that certain varieties of organisms present

FAST FACT . . .

Charles Darwin had a degree in theology – the study of God and religion. This is ironic, considering his later contradictions of their widely held doctrines.

FRST FRCT . . .
Gregor Mendel came up with the rules of heredity wherein he stated that certain characteristic traits get passed on from one generation to another. His ideas were published in 1866, but were not recognized until his death. These rules have helped answer a lot of questions related to humans and their evolution.

on the Galapagos Islands in the Pacific Ocean were also quite independently present elsewhere in similar conditions. This led him to his now famous theories on evolution. He published the controversial and ground breaking "Origin of Species" in 1859.

The book proposed that all life forms came from a common ancestor and evolved step by step to their current forms. This created controversy at that time, since it contradicted the religious beliefs that life was created by an intelligent designer, namely God.

In 1868 he published "The Variation of Animals and Plants Under Domestication," which spoke of selective breeding of animals for particular genetic traits.

Charles Darwin died at 74 and he was buried in Westminster Abbey, fairly near to the tomb of Sir Isaac Newton.

77. JAGADISH CHANDRA BOSE

Among the scientists of the modern times, one of India's most noted brilliant minds is Sir Jagadish Chandra Bose. He is known for his contributions to the field of optics. In spite of not having any exposure to state-of-the-art facilities like other scientists of his period, since he worked in pre-Independence India, he was still able to come up with theories and inventions that were actually 50 years ahead of their time!

Sir Jagadish Chandra Bose was the first well-known scientist of modern India. On returning to India after studies in England, he decided to teach physics as a professor at the Presidency College in Kolkata. He was the first Indian to teach science there.

He carried out research from 1894 onwards on radio waves, so as to make wireless communication equipment. This was around the same time that another great Italian scientist, Marconi, was also carrying out research on the same topic. Bose invented the "iron-mercury-iron coherer with telephone detector," and he became the first person to use semi-conductor junctions to capture radio waves. He also worked on millimeter wavelengths. It is believed that this research was 50 years ahead of his time. There is a lot of debate on the topic of who really invented the radio and a lot of people give him the credit for it. As he was not interested in patenting his inventions and since he was not in proper contact with Marconi, his research in this field has not received the credit.

Sir Bose also carried out important research in the field of biology.

78. GALILEO GALILEI

Born in Pisa on February 15, 1564, Galileo was an Italian physicist, mathematician, astronomer, philosopher, and flautist who played a vital role in the Scientific Revolution. He is credited with the first documented use of the refracting telescope to observe the skies. He is also credited with the founding of observational astronomy and advocacy of the theories of Nicolas Copernicus.

Galileo first heard about the invention of the telescope in Holland in 1609. From the descriptions he heard, he created a vastly improved model and used it to study the skies. By this point, he knew a lot about the fields on kinematics and the motion of uniformly accelerated objects. Once at the University of Padua, he learned of the theory of Heliocentricity proposed by Copernicus. Based on his celestial observations, he wholly agreed with this theory and began teaching it. This became a major point of conflict with the

FAST FACT . . .
Galileo turned blind at the age of 72. Though this was initially suspected to be due to his work with telescopes, it was later revealed to be a result of cataracts and glaucoma.

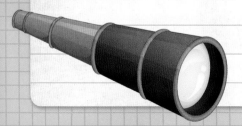

Roman Catholic Church for the rest of his life.

Galileo's greatest contribution to science was his observational approach and the ability to simplify questions that needed to be answered by science. He died under house arrest even though he had been cleared of all charges.

Galileo also studied the pendulum in great detail. Legend has it that he started the study of the pendulum when he saw a lamp in the Cathedral of Pisa continuously oscillate back and forth. Though he came up with several correct theories about pendulums, Galileo was never able to construct a pendulum clock.

FAST FACT . . .

While on his deathbed in 1543, Copernicus presented the theory that the Sun is stationary and at the center of the universe, with the planets revolving around it. This was a great breakthrough as before this, the Earth was considered to be at the center of the universe.

79. JOHANNES KEPLER

Johannes Kepler was born on December 27, 1571, in Weil der Stadt, Swabia, southwest Germany. He is one of the greatest scientists of the Middle Ages. Having battled through an extremely tough childhood, he went on to become a great student of planetary motions. He came up with different scientific laws which, even in modern times, form the basis for studies in physics that are related to planetary motion.

As a child, Kepler led a very unfortunate life. He contracted smallpox at the age of four, which crippled his hands and left his eyesight permanently weakened. In 1576, his family moved to Leonberg. Kepler commenced his education here in a German school, moving to a Latin one later, and went on to attend the University of Tuebingen in 1589 to study theology and philosophy.

Under the guidance of mathematics professor,

Michael Mastlin, Kepler learned about the Ptolemaic and Copernican system of planetary motion. After his education was completed, he moved to Prague as an assistant to Tycho Brahe, royal astronomer and mathematician. Here, he came into conflict with Brahe because Brahe believed in egocentricity and Kepler believed in heliocentricity. When Brahe died, Kepler succeeded him in working for Emperor Rudolph II. Kepler published his famous work "Astronomia Nova" and defined his now legendary three laws of planetary motion.

One interesting fact about Kepler is that he worked and lived around the same time as Galileo. Both these great scientists often disagreed on a lot of facts about science, but their concurrent work really helped spur physics and astronomy rapidly forward toward a new level of understanding.

FAST FACT . . .
Kepler was neither famous nor rich during his lifetime, but his findings led to the discoveries made by Isaac Newton and all the others that followed.

80. MARIE CURIE

Marie Curie was born in Warsaw on November 7, 1867. She was the fifth and the youngest daughter of a secondary school teacher. Along with her husband, Pierre Curie, she redefined the field of science, which is now called radioactivity. One of the most influential women of her generation, she came up with several discoveries and laws for which she is still remembered today.

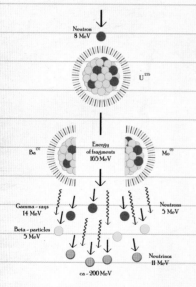

The Nuclear Fission Chain Reaction of a Uranium Atom

Marie Curie received her early education from a local school where her father taught her mathematics and physics – the subjects that Marie was to pursue. In 1894, she met Pierre Curie, instructor in the School of Physics and Chemistry. Marie had begun her scientific career in Paris with an examination of the magnetic properties of various steels; it was this common interest in magnetism that brought Marie and Pierre together. They married in 1895.

In 1896, with Henry Becquerel's discovery of radioactivity, the Curies were inspired to look into uranium rays as a subject for a thesis. In 1898, their brilliant research led to the discovery of "polonium," named after Poland where Marie was born, and radium. In 1903, the Royal Swedish Academy of Sciences honored both Pierre Curie and Marie Curie with the Nobel Prize in Physics for their joint research on radiation.

When Pierre passed away in an untimely manner in 1906, Marie took over his position as Professor of General Physics in the Faculty of Sciences. By 1910, Marie had successfully isolated pure radium. This led to her receiving a second Nobel Prize in 1911, this time in chemistry. With that, she became the first person ever to receive a Nobel Prize in two separate fields of research.

FAST FACT . . .
Marie Curie passed away on July 4, 1934, of a plastic anaemia caused by her exposure to radiation during her work.

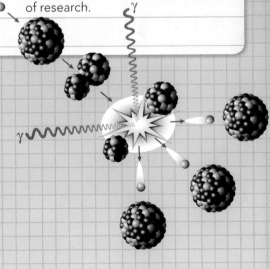

81. MAX PLANCK

Max Karl Ernst Ludwig Planck was born in Kiel, Germany, on April 23, 1858. This German physicist was mainly active in the field of theoretical physics, making many substantial contributions to it. During his time, physicists had started looking for an alternative to quantum physics. Max Planck immortalized himself with his contributions.

Max Planck's fame primarily rests on his role as the originator of quantum theory. Planck's Theory of Quantum Mechanics, along with Einstein's work on relativity in the space time continuum, revolutionized our understanding of time and space.

Planck came up with a formula known as Planck's Radiation Formula to explain a type of electromagnetic radiation by combining the works of Wien and Raleigh. It was during this time, while at the University of Berlin, that Planck came up with his theory of discrete packets of energy known as quanta – thus establishing quantum theory.

The discovery of quantum theory led to the development of a completely new field of physics known as quantum physics. In a way, Planck completely revolutionized the field of physics as he literally founded the field of theoretical physics during a period when it was not actually considered a discipline.

FAST FACT . . .

Music was perhaps Planck's best subject at school, and he was awarded the school prize in catechism and good conduct practically every year.

His discovery of the quantum of action, which is also known as Planck's constant 'h' and is widely used in physics and chemistry, was developed in 1900.

Planck was also interested in the law of conservation of energy and the second law of thermodynamics. His thesis at the University of Munich was based on these theories.

82. JOHN DALTON

There have been many great physicists and chemists in the field of science over the years. The great British chemist, meteorologist, and physicist, John Dalton, is definitely one of them. His efforts led to the development of the modern atomic theory. He was the first person to record color blindness. He carried out detailed research to explain the shortage of color perception.

John Dalton.

John Dalton was extremely interested in studying the cause of color blindness as he suffered from it. He carried out detailed research in this field and found out that discoloration of the eyeball's liquid medium was one of the main reasons for color blindness.

Dalton also developed an interest in meteorology and he maintained daily records of local temperature, wind, humidity, and atmospheric pressure. In 1803, he published a paper on the historic Dalton's Law which stated that the sum of the partial pressure of each

Secondly, the atoms in a particular element are identical. Thirdly, atoms of different elements can be differentiated according to their different atomic weights. Fourthly, atoms of different elements combine during chemical reactions to form chemical compounds in fixed ratios. Lastly, atoms

individual component of a gas mixture is equal to the total pressure exerted by a gaseous mixture. This theory is still used today.

However, Dalton is best known for his atomic theory. There are five main points of his original atomic theory which have continued to remain unchanged. Firstly, the fact that elements are made of the smallest particles called atoms.

FAST FACT . . .

Dalton discovered color blindness. As he suffered from it, he spent a lot of time researching on the reasons for such a condition. As a result, color blindness is also often referred to as "Daltonism."

can neither be created nor destroyed.

COOLER

BOILING POINT

GIZMOS

RADIO

FLOATING

MAGIC

TASTING

EATING

HEAT

DRY

WASH

SCIENCE IN OUR DAILY LIVES

DISSOLVING

ELECTRICITY

WATER

83. RADIO WAVES

Just like light, there are other electromagnetic waves in the electromagnetic spectrum. These are waves of frequencies that are not visible to the human eye but have same type of energy as light. The interesting thing about these waves is that they bounce.

FAST FACT . . .

To create radio waves powerful enough to travel around the world and still be heard, we build giant transmitter disks and put them on top of towers to provide a sufficient range. These towers carry thousands upon thousands of words everyday.

The outermost layer of the Earth's atmosphere, about 53 miles above the surface, is known as the ionosphere. The Sun's radiation falling on the particles there have made them electrically charged. This layer reflects radio waves. As a result, we can bounce radio waves off the ionosphere and send them from one point on Earth to another without much effort. Think of this as having a dark corner in your house where sunlight won't reach. Take a mirror, hold it in front of a beam of sunlight, and reflect that light into the dark corner of the house. In the case of radio waves, your mirror is the ionosphere.

84. HOT!

Have you ever seen a thermos flask? It keeps hot things hot and cold things cold for a specific amount of time. How does it do this?

To understand this, we first have to understand how heat travels. Heat travels in three ways:

Conduction

Objects, generally solids, transmit heat. Heat one end of a metal spoon and the other end starts getting hot.

Convection

In fluids like gases, hot fluid becomes lighter and flows away, while cold fluid flows in to fill the gap. This causes breezes on a hot day. To observe this, put a pot of water to boil and add tiny grains of colored sand or confetti at the bottom. When the water starts to get hot, the confetti flows with the water – demonstrating the flow of convection.

Radiation

Heat is radiated as a wave, like light. Radiated heat is reflected, to a greater or smaller degree, by various objects.

FAST FACT . . .

Radiation is the fastest form of heat transfer, followed by convection, and conduction is the slowest. When you sit next to a fire, you can feel the radiated heat on you even if the air around you is cold.

85. ARCHIMEDES' PRINCIPLE

Archimedes discovered that an object displaced a volume of fluid equal to the volume of the immersed part of the object. This principle, which is referred to as "The Archimedes Principle," led to the development of a basic framework of hydraulic studies in physics.

If you displaced X pounds of fluid, the fluid pushed you up with X pounds of force. These two combine to create something called buoyancy.

The weight of a liquid you displace related to your own determines whether or not you will float. That is why a sheet of metal will sink, but that same sheet beaten into a pan will float. This is the principle used in the making of boats out of steel and other materials that would normally sink.

FAST FACT . . .
Icebergs have nine-tenths of their mass underwater. This is because ice is only a little lighter than water, nine-tenths lighter, to be precise.

This is also how helicopters fly. The fans on top of a helicopter rotate very fast, displacing large amounts of air. This causes the air to push the helicopter, lifting it up.

86. BOILING POINT

Different fluids boil at different temperatures. Water boils at 212°F, alcohol at around 176°F, and gasoline at an even lower temperature. If you take a solution of two liquids that boil at different temperatures and heat it to the boiling point of the one with a lower boiling point, what happens?

Say you have an alcohol-water mixture that is heated to 176°F. The alcohol is boiling away and evaporating, but the water is not.

If you boil away the alcohol, collect the vapors, and cool them, you have successfully separated a mixture of two liquids that dissolve in each other. The same is true for various components of crude oil like diesel, petrol, aviation fuel, naphtha, etc. This process is known as fractional distillation, and commonly referred to as "fracking," like the crude oil is "fracked" to refine it.

FAST FACT . . .

The boiling point of a liquid is not constant – it changes depending on the outside pressure. Water boils at lower than 212°F at a high altitude.

87. SCIENCE OF DRYING

Most of the actions that we perform in daily life are a form of science experiments. Science has an explanation for almost everything. Our basic household chores are influenced by science in some way or another. Let's take the example of drying clothes and see how this is also a scientific phenomena caused by atmospheric conditions and scientific processes.

Do you ever wonder how your washed clothes dry? Have you given a thought to why your clothes are spread out and exposed to sunlight to dry them? Such occurrences are so common in our daily lives that we don't even bother thinking about them! The reason why clothes dry is due to a scientific phenomenon called evaporation.

When clothes are washed, they get wet. In other words, the pores in the clothes get filled with water droplets. When we dry clothes, we try and get rid of these water droplets. Once clothes are washed, we wring the clothes to remove as much water as possible. The removal of water by the process of wringing is caused due to the scientific phenomena called inertia.

To get rid of the smaller water droplets and completely dry the clothes, they are spread out and exposed to sunlight or a source of heat. This causes the phenomenon of evaporation to take place.

The water droplets in clothes get converted into water vapor

FAST FACT . . .

The process of evaporation is strictly a surface phenomenon. This means that conversion from water to water vapor starts from the surface and moves downwards from there. This is why evaporation differs from boiling, which takes place throughout the entire bulk of the liquid.

and escape into the atmosphere. The clothes are thus free from the water droplets and therefore dry. Think about this the next time you wash your clothes and hang them out to dry.

88. EATING

Eating is second nature to us. We simply pick up whatever food we want to eat and put it into our mouths. We then wait for it to get digested and excrete the unwanted food substances from our body. Have you ever wondered what actually happens inside the body? The process of digestion in the digestive system is a complex procedure!

Our body has different systems that perform different functions. Among them, the digestive system is one of the most important ones. Responsible for all the ice cream, cookies, vegetables, and vitamins that we eat, it deals with each of these foods differently and ensures that they get digested. This is how it works…

The digestive system starts working even before we actually take in the food. When we see the food and smell it, saliva starts building up in our mouth which prepares it for the food that is going to be taken in. Once we begin to eat, the saliva works on the food to break down the chemicals in it and make it soft. Food in this condition is also referred to as "bolus." The tongue then assists in pushing the food in small portions to the back of our throats and into the esophagus, which is the second part of the digestive tract.

From there on, the nutrients and energy that we get from the food are obtained by breaking down the food in different steps in the other parts of the digestive system. This includes the small intestine, the large intestine, and the stomach. Who would've known that the simple act of eating food could be such a complex procedure?

FAST FACT . . .

If it was opened and spread out, the digestive system is around 30 feet long from the mouth to the anus. That's around 5-6 times taller than we actually are!

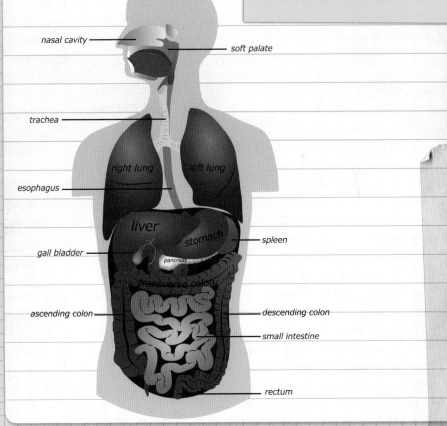

nasal cavity

soft palate

trachea

right lung

left lung

esophagus

liver

stomach

spleen

gall bladder

pancreas

transverse colon

ascending colon

descending colon

small intestine

rectum

89. SUGAR, SUGAR!

Sugar and salt are the most common ingredients in our diet. When we drink tea or milk, we add some sugar cubes or use sugar powder to sweeten it. Salt is a very important ingredient in almost every type of food that we eat. Do you notice how sugar and salt never appear in their actual form in the food we eat? They seem to disappear.

The reason why we can't see the sugar or salt that we add to our food is due to the phenomena of dissolution. When we add a cube of sugar or sugar powder into milk or tea and stir it, the sugar particles get dissolved into it. When they dissolve, they simply become a part of the solution without losing their basic properties. Thus, although we are unable to see the sugar particles, they still continue to impart the sweet taste that they are used for.

If we continue adding sugar or salt to a glass of water and keep stirring it, we will observe that

the sugar or salt particles will dissolve initially but stop doing so after a certain period of time. They will simply remain in the glass, suspended at the bottom.

This is because a given quantity of solution has a particular tendency to dissolve another substance. As we keep adding sugar and it keeps dissolving, it reaches a point where no more sugar will dissolve at the given temperature and pressure. At this point, the solution is called a saturated solution.

FAST FACT . . .

By changing conditions such as temperature or pressure, it is possible to dissolve more particles of a certain type than would actually be present under normal conditions of temperature and pressure. A solution of this type is referred to as a super saturated solution.

90. CAN YOU TASTE IT?

The words "taste" and "flavor" are often used interchangeably. We generally use the word "flavor" when we are at an ice cream place or a frozen yogurt joint, trying to decide which flavor of ice cream we would like to buy. It is interesting to note how we never talk about the taste of the ice cream we decide to buy. Scientifically, taste and flavor are quite different as concepts.

Taste is one of the five senses that every human being possesses, along with touch, smell, hearing, and vision. It is one of our five sensory organs. The tongue possesses various taste buds that are responsible for sensing the flavor of different foods. These sensory perceptions can be credited to the taste buds in our mouth and how they make us perceive different types of food.

Though we believe that taste and flavor are the same thing, they are actually very different. Flavor does not simply involve the taste of a particular food item. It also makes use of our other senses like smell and vision. The flavor of a particular food item is not simply determined by the way it tastes. Apart from the taste, the way a particular food looks and

FAST FACT . . .

As we keep growing older, the number of taste buds in our mouth keeps reducing. Babies have the maximum number of taste buds. This means that the older we grow, the more we lose out on the taste of the food!

the way it smells also add to its flavor. So, the flavor of strawberry ice cream is not just decided by the taste of strawberry which we receive from it, but also by the way it looks and the way it smells.

You can always remember that a food with a good flavor might not always be tasty!

FAST FACT . . .

Some creatures which use different biological processes to sense different things. Butterflies, for instance, taste things with their hind feet! Their sense of taste is based on touch. They touch different leaves to figure out whether they are edible or not, and also taste them. Imagine tasting food with your feet.

91. CENTER OF GRAVITY

Gravity is arguably the most important force on the face of Earth. It is because of gravity that we remain grounded. In the absence of it, we would be floating, just like astronauts in outer space. It is one of the unique features of planet Earth which differentiates it from every other planet in our solar system. An interesting fundamental related to gravity is the center of gravity.

Gravity as a force acts equally on every single body on Earth. As long as we work the way that it wants us to, life is much easier. But the moment we try to work against it, things get tougher.

Let's understand this with an example.

Walking down the stairs always seems to be easier than walking up the stairs. This is because when we are walking down the stairs, we are walking in the direction of gravity. However, when we walk up the stairs, we move against the direction of gravity. This means that we are actually fighting against it to make our way up. It's similar to someone pinning us down to the ground while we try to

FAST FACT . . .

Due to the absence of gravity, there is no way that astronauts can cry in space as the tear droplets cannot roll down their cheeks, even though their tear ducts are functional.

grapple to stand up and escape the hold. If the force we exert in the direction opposite to that of gravity is not greater than the force of gravity, we won't be able to act against it. Luckily for us, we can act against it, which is why we can climb up the stairs and climb mountains. The concept of the center of gravity is very important in determining the orientation of objects for smooth motion.

FAST FACT . . .

Quite contrary to popular belief, Velcro was not actually discovered as a part of the American space program. It was discovered by a Swiss engineer who was walking his dog. On returning home, he realized that both his clothes and his dog were covered in burrs. He carried out detailed research on this and developed Velcro as a result.

92. CHEMICALLY ENGULFED

While biology controls the functioning of all living objects, chemistry is another important branch of science present all around us. Everything in the world is a chemical. The book you are reading is made of different chemicals. Your bed could be made of wood which consists of carbon and other important materials. Similarly, everything in the world is made up of chemicals! It would be interesting to note what different things around us are actually composed of.

The science of chemistry is the study of different chemicals, their properties, and behavior. As mentioned earlier, everything around us is made of chemicals. Milk that forms an important part of most of our diets consists of a chemical called lactic acid. Sugar has carbohydrates and fats. Oranges and lemons have large quantities of citric acid. Plastic is a common constituent

FAST FACT . . .

The Last Element in the Periodic Table
Newer elements keep getting discovered all the time and then become a part of the periodic table. At present there are 118 elements in the periodic table with the last element at present having an atomic number of 118 and called "ununoctium."

of different objects used in daily life. It belongs to family of chemicals called polymers. Buckets that we use to collect water or to have a bath are made up of teflon, which is an important polymer. Even the floors of our houses and our schools are combinations of different chemicals. Wooden floors consist of carbon and different elements, while marble floors consist of a chemical called limestone, which is rich in calcium.

Chemists and scientists keep trying to create newer chemicals from existent ones to serve different purposes. There are different industrial methods that are commonly used for chemical production. For example, the contact process is used to manufacture sulfuric acid, while the Haber's process is used to manufacture ammonia. There are many other processes used to manufacture different chemicals.

Haber

93. HARD WATER

You will notice that it is easier to have a bath in certain places as compared to others. This is because the properties of water differ from place to place, depending on the different chemicals that form a part of it. Based on these chemicals, it is difficult to take a bath in certain types of water.

In order for us to comfortably have a bath with soap, it is very important for the soap to lather up. This is totally dependent on the type of water. Broadly, water is divided into two categories, hard water and soft water. Soft water is the type of water which is easier to have a bath with, as it ensures that soap lathers easily.

Hard water has different properties as compared to soft water. This is due to the difference in the minerals that are present in it. Calcium, magnesium, and their compounds are present in larger amounts in hard water as compared to soft water. This gives hard water a bigger advantage in certain cases, but makes it disadvantageous in the case of having a bath, which is a little inconvenient!

Hard water can be converted into soft water through several different processes. Different parts of the world have different chemical constituents present in water. Based on this, a particular type of water might be hard or soft in nature. One of the disadvantages of hard water is that it leaves deposits called "scales" in water pipes, which cause damage to them.

FAST FACT . . .

Roughly 70 percent of the Earth is made up of water. It is interesting to note that only 3 percent of the world's total water content is available for our use. The sources of this are groundwater aquifers, rivers, and freshwater lakes.

94. SURFACE TENSION

Surface tension is a very important scientific phenomenon responsible for different interesting daily life occurrences. This is the reason why we often see certain substances separating from each other, due to which some living species like insects can walk over water while we can't!

Surface tension is the tendency of a fluid's surface to contract, which gives it the ability to resist an external force. This phenomenon is responsible for ensuring that certain objects float on water even though their density is greater than that of water. This is why certain living species like water striders are able to walk over water. Surface tension affects many different daily occurrences.

Let us take the example of water droplets or dew drops on leaves. When the moisture in the atmosphere condenses early in the morning, they

combine to form beads on leaves. This spherical shape that the water droplets take up is due to surface tension.

Different liquids differ in their surface tension. For example, oil and water have different surface tensions. This is why when oil and water are mixed, they always separate. If you observe

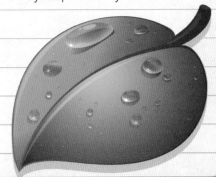

milk closely, you will observe transparent oil droplets on the surface. This is because the oil separates from the water content in the milk due to different surface tensions.

It's a very important concept in science, which is also responsible for soup being a lot tastier when it's warmer as compared to when it turns cold.

FAST FACT . . .

Ordinary soap bubbles are always unstable in water as they have a large surface area and a small mass. The addition of surfactants stabilizes them as they greatly reduce the surface tension.

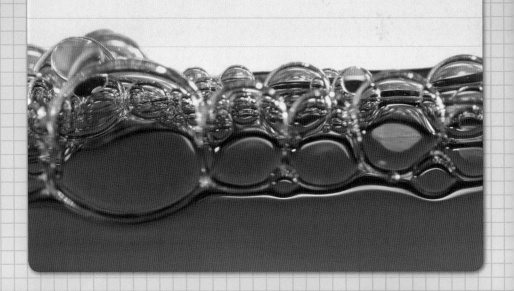

95. PRESSURE COOKER

Pressure cookers are important pieces of equipment that make the process of cooking easier. This interesting equipment makes use of the relation between temperature, boiling point, and pressure, which speeds up the time taken to cook different types of food. Pressure cookers are particularly important when cooking at high altitudes.

There is a very interesting relation between pressure and temperature. Boiling point is the temperature at which a liquid gets converted into a gas. It is easier to cook different foods in liquid form as compared to gaseous form. As altitudes increase, the pressure increases, which makes cooking tougher. That is where the pressure cooker works as a savior!

Pressure cookers are used to cook food under higher pressures because at that level, the boiling point also increases. It is easier to cook foods in liquid form as compared to gaseous form. Since the pressure increases, which also results in the boiling points increasing, food remains

in its liquid form up to higher temperatures, which makes cooking it faster.

Pressure cookers are commonly used at higher altitudes for this purpose, where cooking is made a lot tougher due to reduced boiling points. The use of the pressure cooker increases the boiling point, which ensures that different types of foods can be cooked. This wouldn't have been possible at lower temperatures without the pressure cooker.

FAST FACT . . .

Blood pressure is also a very important part of our human body. It is important to keep our blood pressure between acceptable limits to lead a healthy life.

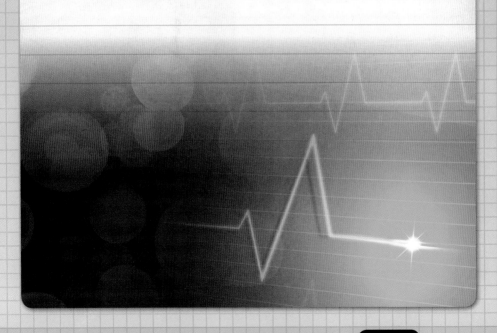

96. WEIRD WATER

Water is a very interesting compound that behaves differently in different cases. While all substances uniformly follow a certain change in temperature, water is very different. Between a certain set of temperatures, water has a unique behavior pattern.

All substances in the world expand on heating and contract on cooling. When we raise their temperature, substances seem to appear bigger. When we lower the temperature, they seem to appear smaller. A very common example of this can be seen in the case of an airbag. When we heat the airbag, the gas inside it expands, which makes the airbag grow bigger. When we cool it, the gas inside contracts and makes it appear smaller.

Water, on the other hand, is extremely different. Between 32°F and 39°F, it behaves in a completely opposite manner. On heating up to 32°F from negative temperatures, water first expands. However, between 32°F and 39°F, it contracts on raising the temperature rather than expanding. After 39°F, it starts expanding normally like all other substances do. Similarly, on cooling up to 39°F, it contracts, after which it starts expanding up to 32°F instead of contracting like all other substances. Beyond 32°F, it behaves just like all other substances. This behavior of water is also called the anomalous behavior. It is due to this that the density of water is affected and ice floats over water.

FAST FACT . . .
Water is made up of two atoms of hydrogen and one atom of water. Therefore its chemical name is H_2O.

97. GIZMOS

Today, it is almost impossible to imagine life without the dozen odd tech-products that we are so accustomed to using. They are like a lifeline for us. Right from cell phones to computers and tablets, it is impossible to imagine our lives without them. They make life easier and, more importantly, we have come to depend on them!

Science has made life easier and more sophisticated. Today, the first thing that we probably do when we wake up in the morning is check our cell phones for missed calls or messages. We spend a lot of time watching different shows on television. The computer is like our best friend, because we spend hours completing our projects and assignments on it. And of course, we have the Internet! Life would have been impossible for us in its absence.

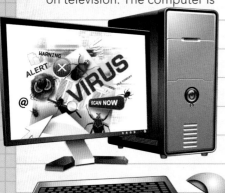

FAST FACT . . .

One thing that all of us dread and really dislike is a computer virus. We all detest them. However, various mischievous and brainy people keep developing them. There are over 6,000 computer viruses in circulation every single month!

Scientists are responsible for developing technology to the level that it is today. While the development of computers started in the 1800s with Charles Babbage, pioneers like Bill Gates of Microsoft and Steve Jobs of Apple have made these one of the most important gizmos in modern life.

Computer science is the branch of science that deals with the coding and development of these devices. It has undergone massive advancements and is continuing to undergo more developments on a daily basis. From a time when computers were the size of buildings, we now have computers, laptops, and tablets that are smaller than the size of our palms! Can you imagine how this will progress in the years to come?

FAST FACT . . .

Over the years, the Internet has really grown and spread to different parts of the world. By the end of 2012, a staggering 17 billion devices were connected to the Internet.

Bill Gates

Steve Jobs

98. ELECTRICITY AND POWER

Electricity is important for everything we do today. Right from watching television to studying in the night, it is impossible to do any of these things without electric power. Electricity can be generated by various different methods. As the major sources of electricity have started to deplete now, it is important that we start looking at alternate sources to produce it.

Electricity is our lifeline in modern times. Imagining life without electricity is close to impossible! Electricity has traditionally been produced by making use of coal, petroleum, and recently, natural gas. However, these are non-renewable sources of energy. In other words, they will get exhausted in the course of time. Hence, it is very important for us to look for alternative sources of energy that are more viable and help us generate electricity more easily.

FAST FACT . . .

Water and metals are good conductors of electricity. If you decide to use an electronic device while bathing, you could get an electric shock!

Solar energy, which is basically the energy from the Sun, is widely used for electricity generation. Solar panels are set up to obtain electric energy. Since energy from the Sun is unlimited, it is an infinite source of electric energy. Using the tides of seas and the flow of wind to generate electricity is also very common. In areas with a lot of greenery and on the outskirts of cities, we can see windmills that generate electricity using wind.

Electricity can also be generated from human waste and other different chemicals. At present, a lot of research is being carried out into generating electricity using renewable sources.

99. SCIENCE AND MAGIC

Everything that appears magical to us is actually making smart use of science. All magicians come up with their tricks by making use of different scientific applications. Science can almost entirely be credited for the development and popularity of the art of magic.

Every magician would like to claim that everything they perform is due to the special powers they possess. However, their special powers are the knowledge of how to use science to their advantage.

We often hear about different tricks being performed by magicians in which they make a huge structure disappear for a few seconds or how they disappear from one place and suddenly appear in another place. These are optical illusions that make us see things which actually don't exist. Magicians put in a lot of effort in mastering this art, so they can actually be considered to be great students of science. Making use of scientific contraptions, optical illusions, and chemical reactions, they have been able to leave us puzzled since centuries!

For example, though metals have a higher density than water and are supposed to fall to the base of containers full of water, magicians often make metals float on it. They actually make use of the scientific phenomena of surface tension to make this happen.

So it can be safely said that the secret to magic is nothing but science!

FAST FACT . . .
There is enough salt in oceans to cover all the continents up to a depth of 500 feet!

100. BLOBS IN A BOTTLE

There are many interesting scientific experiments that can be easily conducted at home, creating very beautiful results. A great experiment that would give you a wonderful decorative piece would be the "blobs in a bottle" experiment. You can have beautiful, colorful blobs that appear at different points in a bottle.

First pour water into a decently shaped bottle, say a soda bottle. Do not fill it to the brim. Pour vegetable oil through a measuring cup or funnel into the bottle until it is almost full. Now, wait for the water and the oil to separate out.

Add some food coloring agent to the bottle. Choose any color you like. The drops will pass through the oil and mix with the water below. Take half a fizzing tablet, drop it into the bottle, and watch it sink to the bottom. You will observe blobs form all of a sudden that are very attractive. You can add the other half of the tablet to keep the effect going. If you want the effect of a lava lamp, all you need to do is shine a flashlight through the bottom of the bottle.

This phenomenon is actually scientific in nature and depends on different concepts such as surface tension, reflection, refraction, and, most importantly, the difference in density between oil and water.

FAST FACT . . .
There are 62,000 blood vessels in the human body. If they were to be laid end to end, they would circle the Earth 2.5 times!

101. AUTOMOBILES

Transport is impossible to imagine without cars, motorbikes, trains, buses, and airplanes. It would be interesting to note that these too are gifts that science has given to us! As science keeps progressing, we have moved from the times of the basic cars that were common in the 1940s to absolutely sophisticated high-end cars that we use today!

Cars are scientific marvels. Everything about them is related to science – right from the motion of their wheels and how they make use of friction to the hydraulic systems which help us brake or accelerate. Even the conversion of energy and the functioning of car engine are purely governed by science. Cars have evolved greatly over the years. Studying one model and how it functions in detail would be a huge science project in itself, which would last for over a year. Several branches of science such as kinematics, hydraulics, and chemistry are used in the making of cars. The next time you see a Ferrari buzzing past you, remember to thank science for it!

INDEX